THE
ADHD
FIX

15 STRATEGIES YOU NEED TO USE TO ACHIEVE YOUR TRUE POTENTIAL

BY

DR. HENRY J. SVEC

&

JOSHUA G. SVEC B.A. M.A.

THE ADHD FIX

15 STRATEGIES YOU NEED TO USE TO ACHIEVE YOUR TRUE POTENTIAL

Copyright © 2016 by Henry Svec

Cover design and interior layout | Yvonne Parks | www.PearCreative.ca
Editing | Alethea Spiridon Hopson | www.freelanceeditor.ca

ISBN 978-0-9684275-1-4

DEDICATION

This book is dedicated to my father Jindroh (Henry). He taught us by example, through his fight and escape from the Czech Republic, to always battle for what you believe, never quit the fight, and the value of education applied through common sense.

TABLE OF CONTENTS

FOREWORD

It was 1974 and I was sitting in the guidance office at Oakridge Secondary School in London, Ontario. Kemper, as he was called, not only dabbled in guidance and physical education, but also coached the golf team. He was laid back, rarely displaying any anger or frustration over the usual pranks pulled daily at the school. He started our conversation that day by asking me how I was doing, what was new, how the football team was looking, and other pleasant chatter. Then he got to the reason for my being pulled out of class.

"Since you started here in grade 9, Henry, your grades have been going down steadily—from 85 percent, to 74 percent, to 71 percent, to 68 percent this year. What's going on?"

I had no clue. I thought I was doing very well on the athletic field and in gym, and doing even better socially. I told him I would promise to work hard; he was pleased and let me go. I graduated my final year of high school with a 61 percent and was miraculously accepted at the University of Western Ontario.

I didn't know it back then, and wouldn't know it for some thirty-four years, but I had undiagnosed ADHD. I also had a learning disability with some very specific pockets of giftedness. My grades in high school were slipping because not being able to focus, poor organizational skills, and an inability to get my thoughts on paper started to take their toll. At one point, many thought I had experienced mild traumatic brain injury from my high school and college football career, but later experts told me it was ADHD.

Years of trial and error taught me how to overcome academic obstacles. I earned a bachelor's degree in physical and health education, a bachelor's degree in education, a master's degree in education, and in 1988 a Ph.D. from Michigan State University. Wonder what my high school guidance counselor would say about that, or perhaps the professor from the University of Western Ontario who told me in 1977 that I didn't have the brains or what it took to be in his program. I could tell you many more such stories, but you get the picture. ADHD-oppositional behavior is helpful when you're surrounded by idiots who keep trying to tear you down by telling you your goals are unrealistic.

As a psychologist, I have spent the past twenty years helping others develop tools and strategies to overcome many ADHD obstacles so they too can achieve success. During that time, I have also learned valuable lessons to maximize my own performance, tools I will share in this book. It has taken me many years to fully understand my own condition. Only within the past ten years, due to ever-improving technologies, have I been able to identify ADHD, various learning disabilities, and gifted behavior.

The most significant development has been the use of neuroimaging (or a brain scan or QEEG) that is reviewed by a neurologist and brain physiologist to help identify if neurological or brain patterns exist for types of ADHD. I've had many scans done on my own brain by some of the world's most respected authorities. In the early years when I was training, volunteers were often asked to step up to have an image done. I would insist on being that subject, which has taught me many valuable lessons and also provided me with world-class clinical opinions of my brain. The images provided at different locations with different types of equipment pointed to the same conclusion and confirmed my diagnosis.

The purpose of this book is to help you find your ADHD success, to learn to live with it and even enjoy it and the unexpected gifts it brings. ADHD is a gift that, if nurtured and properly fine-tuned, will allow you to achieve well beyond your non-diagnosed colleagues and friends. You will likely discover that other learning style issues, giftedness, or specific learning disabilities are also part of who you are. Most important is that you will learn how to live with ADHD success instead of failure.

The ADHD "fix" is about using proven strategies to eliminate the negative impact of ADHD symptoms on the life of a child, teen, or adult. Traditionally, health care professionals try to find ways to make the individual with ADHD fit into existing environments or structures. The ADHD Fix is about creating strategies or a "toolbox" of solutions that if used and modified throughout a lifetime will change the environment to fit the ADHD lifestyle. ADHD is a life-long condition; just like medication, if you stop using these strategies, the ADHD symptoms will again return and negatively impact your life.

Let's get started.

STRATEGY 1
RELEASE THE STIGMA

Having ADHD can mean many things. You will learn in a later chapter of this book how it is a gift, one that will place you well above others in your classroom or profession. But in excess of 60 percent of those with ADHD (when asked) will state that they feel a stigma or fear of others finding out about their condition. It is a common feeling.

Humans, unfortunately, have for centuries felt the need to discriminate against groups of people that are a bit different from the majority. We have moved forward on many fronts, as education and knowledge overcomes bias and prejudice. The stigma of ADHD can, however, stop someone from seeking out a proper assessment or treatment for their condition. Many adults report they don't consult with a psychologist or their doctor about their symptoms for fear of this stigma.

Accept the diagnosis

If you or your child has had a comprehensive assessment you will feel more confident in the diagnosis and subsequent strategy plan. For children and teens, do a quick search on the web and read about famous people with the diagnosis of ADHD. You will find examples in every walk of life.

Live in quiet confidence

Having ADHD doesn't mean you shout it out to the rafters and tell someone after a short two-minute conversation. Yes, teachers and professors need to know right away, but what about your employer? If you have worked on the strategies in this book and are beginning to see positive gains, it may or may not be appropriate to tell your boss. Consider the benefits of disclosing:

> ➤ Will it allow you to use certain strategies or tools within the workplace to enhance your productivity and success?

> ➤ Are you required by law to disclose your condition or treatments you may be taking?

Living in quiet confidence means you have your internal house in order, understand your condition, and are beginning to apply the strategies you need to be successful.

Focus on the gifted aspects of ADHD

Creativity, spontaneity, controlled impulses, outgoing personality, energy, and intelligence are all characteristics of someone with ADHD. Often these may be hidden from view due to a number of factors that we will discuss in this book. Remember, they are within your grasp and are positive aspects of ADHD.

KEY IDEA FROM THIS STRATEGY

With the diagnosis of ADHD often follows the stigma of "what will others think?" This is a process to help you achieve your potential in all aspects of your life: better relationships with others, better performance at work, and being more successful as a parent and partner are all within your grasp. Accepting that you, or someone you love, has ADHD is a major step in this process.

STRATEGY 2
ASK WHO IS POINTING THE FINGER?

For children, it's primarily their teachers who point the finger and say something is wrong with them. In extreme cases, parents may be the first to notice that their child isn't like others. For young adults in senior high school or university, it is parents who will point the finger, saying school performance isn't what it should be. Sometimes during the early college or university years, the bottom falls out and the student fails. For older adults, it is usually the spouse, or in some cases the employer, who points the finger. Let's look at each one of these and what you need to know before you listen to the "experts."

Children and teachers

Despite what you may think, teachers get into their profession because they want to help children. Some do think of the summers off, the salary and benefits, but the demands in the classroom require the profession to only keep passionate, dedicated, hard-working teachers. Unions have somewhat diluted that concept, so the few incompetent, uncaring, and unprofessional ones are kept in the classroom. This becomes a problem if your child with ADHD is in a class with such a teacher.

The real issue when a teacher tells you they think your child has ADHD is their lack of training to make that determination.

I attended teachers college in 1978 to earn my bachelor's degree in education, a process that took a grand total of eight months, and then ten weeks in a real classroom. You need more hands-on training in Ontario to be a butcher, hair stylist, plumber, or electrician.

When I graduated from Michigan State University in 1988 with my Ph.D., I went back to teachers college to teach the teachers. I needed the money after spending two years as an adult student with two young children. At that time, taking my class in school psychology, or educational psychology, was an option, which meant that you could graduate teachers college without any knowledge of giftedness, special education, or ADHD. While the length of time in the classroom for hands-on training has improved over the years, the lack of formal training regarding ADHD continues.

Teachers have no business diagnosing ADHD. If a principal tells you that your child needs to be on medication to attend his or her school, they are overstepping their authority and possibly breaking the law.

Teachers can provide you with valuable information on what they are seeing in the classroom, on the playground, or in the gym, but that is it. Ask your child's teacher to become involved in the data gathering and observation stage of the assessment process, but only consider the information provided as 5 percent of what you need to help with a proper diagnosis. Some teachers report behavior that is consistent with what they think about your child, your family, and your socioeconomic status. Take anything they tell you with a grain of salt.

You, the parent

You know your child. You watch them at play, in church or synagogue, in sports, the band, dance class, at meals, with their friends or siblings, and on trips. You understand what they are doing, how they learn, and perhaps some alarm bells are ringing. You aren't sure, but think something may be wrong.

That is all you need. I call that the **parental instinct**. It's a feeling. You want to know answers, and want to make sure everything is fine.

You need to listen to those instincts and feelings. If someone else is pointing the finger, take that seriously, because even if nothing is going on, even if your child does not have ADHD, they will treat your child differently—unless you can prove they are wrong. Often in my practice we help parents and educators understand that a child may be gifted, or have a specific learning disability, as well as other challenges that have nothing to do with ADHD. At other times, we find evidence that supports the diagnosis, but that is also a relief because **a plan of success can be developed**. Your job as a parent is to do everything you can to help your child.

Your college-aged child may prove to be a special challenge. Many still feel the stigma of being diagnosed with ADHD, and this fear will stop them from getting help. My son Joshua, the co-author of this book, talks candidly about his experiences in the final chapter. Providing support and coaching for the challenges that your child is facing may be the first step in getting them help.

While it is important to know the actual diagnosis as the first step in getting the right approach, coaching and counseling can help your adult child break through their perceived stigma, and understand that a comprehensive assessment is the first step.

Spouse or partner

Undiagnosed ADHD can be a threat to any relationship because the behavior and perceived disinterest is interpreted by the non-ADHD spouse as a lack of interest in the relationship and person, as a lack of commitment, and a personal attack. Once diagnosed, proper strategies can be developed to help both partners understand and take care of these issues. I have included the Severity Scale for Adult ADHD in the appendix of this book for your review. Do the survey and see if further assessment or evaluation would be helpful.

Your employer

You are having a hard time at work. It is difficult to focus, to concentrate, to organize your day. You find yourself self-medicating, using coffee or other over-the-counter products and high energy drinks to keep your edge. You tire and bore easily. Employer's often point the finger by saying performance is declining. Missing deadlines or a disorganized work area may be an initial clue.

Anger management issues, or open frustrations expressed inappropriately, may also be a sign of undiagnosed ADHD.

Just like the child on the playground, adult ADHD is often only suggested when a crisis is present. Problems at an office party, on a sales trip, in a staff meeting, or an inappropriate confrontation with a co-worker may all result in a referral for diagnosis.

From pointing the finger to diagnosis

If you look at the simple diagram below, you will notice that at the top we have "ADHD Speculation" and at the bottom "ADHD Diagnosis." As you move down the path of assessment you can be sure that the diagnosis is accurate. In the appendix of this book you will find the ADHD Severity Scale (Children), ADHD Severity Scale (Adult), and the ADHD Severity Scale (Athlete). It should be one of the first tools you use to review the severity of the ADHD symptoms that you are seeing. I believe it is the severity of the symptoms that will be an important beginning step in the diagnostic process. Feel free to print them out, or go to our practice web site www.drsvec.com where you will find them under the "Forms" section.

ASSESSMENT CHART

ADHD speculation --->

Teacher comments, problems at school, observations of not
focusing in class -->

Observations on the playground, referral to doctor --------------->

Brief checklist, 5 minute observation ------------------------------->
(where most people stop)

Diagnosis based on poor information ------------------------------->

Screening for other medical causes ------------------------------->

Review of developmental history ----------------------------------->

Comprehensive assessment including Gifted Potential, Learning
Disability, Central Auditory Processing, Emotional Issues and
Neurological Consultation including a brain scan ------------------>

KEY IDEA FROM THIS STRATEGY

- Teachers may often point the finger that something is wrong with your child, but they are not trained to assess, or diagnose, ADHD.

- While checklists and a five-minute interview are often used to complete the assessment, this is not enough.

- A comprehensive assessment is needed. Start with the ADHD Severity Scales located in the appendix of this book.

STRATEGY 3
GET A COMPLETE ASSESSMENT

Before an assessment for ADHD, make sure that all possible medical explanations for what you are seeing have been ruled out. For children, take your child to the pediatrician and ask, "Other than ADHD, are there any other medical reasons for why my child may be having problems concentrating or......" Once the proper medical screening has been completed, and other medical conditions are ruled out, you are ready for an ADHD assessment. Here is what should happen:

- ➤ A history

- ➤ Behavioral checklist

- ➤ Screening for Central Auditory Processing problems

- ➤ How you or the person being tested performs during boring tasks

- ➤ Intelligence testing to determine learning style

- ➤ Achievement testing

- ➤ A brain scan

Get a good history

The psychologist will ask you a number of questions about possible birth complications, early development, and school history. The history should include a review of other family members with ADHD (and go back as far as you can), as well as a clinical interview to determine if other factors may be contributing to the symptoms other than ADHD. Ruling out mild traumatic brain injury, for example, is important when assessing young athletes engaged in contact sports.

Completion of behavior checklists

Checklists will provide a standard way to ask different questions about what symptoms are present and how they are affecting daily functioning. For children and adults, I prefer to use the checklists located in appendix B and C. The questions result in a severity index, which gives an idea of how the presenting symptoms are impacting function. Many times only teachers complete checklists and this alone is not a valid measurement in determining ADHD. Teacher input for children should only account for 0 to 5 percent of the information used to determine the diagnosis of ADHD.

Screening for Central Auditory Processing problems

Central Auditory Processing difficulty (CAP) can often mimic the symptoms of ADHD. Many children and adults with ADHD also have CAP. A screening test is done at the psychologist's office that takes about twenty-five to thirty minutes to complete. A positive finding often results in a referral to an audiologist knowledgeable about CAP.

Performance during very boring tasks

A number of continuous performance measures are used to determine how you or your child will perform on a very boring task. Your performance is then compared to others with or without ADHD. These tests, such as the Connors Continuous Performance Test (CPT), take approximately 15 minutes to complete. The analysis of your results by the psychologist can take a greater amount of time to be able to better understand how you perform when doing boring tasks in a quiet environment. I often wonder if a child or adult is having extreme difficulty completing the CPT in such a quiet office setting, how do they function when faced with such tasks in a busy classroom, or office/work setting?

Intelligence testing to investigate learning style

Traditional intelligence testing, such as the Wechsler Intelligence Scales for children, are administered to understand how new material is learned. The testing is combined with other tools of measurement to determine if a gifted profile may also be present. Children and adults with gifted behavior often look to be ADHD if they are not in an environment that is challenging or interesting. Learning disabilities are also identified using these results, combined with achievement and other testing. I tell children that this testing is about finding out the horse power "under the hood" of the car to see how fast they can go.

Achievement testing

This is about finding out how fast the car is in fact going. We test to determine grade scores (at what grade level someone is reading or writing at, for example) and standard scores (how they compare to others the same age), which can be compared accurately to the intellectual testing. Often, at this point, the information from testing and history gathering may point to a specific learning disability, gifted profile, CAP, or some other life event that is contributing to the problems noted.

The brain scan

While this is just one test of many that is reviewed to determine the diagnosis of ADHD, I believe it is one of the most important. ADHD is a neurological condition. If you don't look at the brain, how do you know if it exists?

At our offices, we use the QEEG or Quantitative Electro Encephalogram. The information generated by the test is reviewed by a neurologist and expert in brain physiology. A number of doctors and scientists believe that there are many different "types" of ADHD, which can only be accurately determined by looking at the brain image. Deregulation in the prefrontal area of the brain may cause different symptoms than deregulation in the temporal regions.

Other neurological conditions, although rare, may also be identified from the QEEG. In a rare case at our offices, petite mal seizure activity was identified during one of our evaluations for ADHD, which resulted in a very different treatment path and level of understanding. This young adult had already been incorrectly diagnosed with ADHD, but luckily his parents wanted a second opinion. Yes, this is a rare diagnosis, but fortunately the parents in this case listened to their instincts and asked us to do a comprehensive evaluation.

Data analysis and report

Once the above tests are completed, a report is written incorporating all of the information identified in the assessment. The report is written for you to use to get the best treatment and programs to achieve success. When I started in practice, schools would sometimes call complaining that my recommendations were unrealistic. They would say that ADHD is a medical, not school, condition and therefore teachers and principals weren't required to accommodate children or teens with the diagnosis.

In response to these calls, I wrote the Premier of Ontario and sometime later received a letter from the Minister of Education who said this among other things:

> "You have also indicated that elementary and secondary schools are not providing support to students with a diagnosis of ADHD. School boards have obligations under the Ontario Human Rights Code to accommodate students with ADHD since the Ontario Human Rights Commission regards ADHD as a disability; therefore, such students have protections under the Code. In elementary and secondary schools, the duty to accommodate is met by the provision of special education programs and services."

We posted the entire letter on our website www.drsvec.com so parents could print it and take it with them should they need to advocate at the school level.

As our testing procedures become more exact, it is more common to see a combination of factors impacting a persons learning and performance, as opposed to a single diagnosis of ADHD. This comprehensive testing is capable of pinpointing "flavors" of issues as I call them. The problem is that once identified, what does a school and parent do with someone with ADHD-Inattentive Type + Mild Disorder of Expressive Language + Gifted Profile in the Perceptual Visual domain?

We will get to that in later chapters, but the first challenge is to **be comfortable with the assessment.** As a parent, you want to do all that you can to help your child. If you suspect that your child has ADHD, there are no shortcuts. A comprehensive assessment is necessary.

As an adult with ADHD, you want to make sure the diagnosis is clear and understandable.

A diagnosis of depression, or anxiety disorder with ADHD, is often seen with adults assessed at our offices. Was depression part of a neurological pattern that was present with the ADHD, or did depression occur as a result of negative experiences and a reaction to untreated ADHD? This is an important distinction. If you believe that the depression was always there, then perhaps treating it with medication may make more sense than if the condition was brought about by secondary reactions to the ADHD condition.

The type of ADHD you have should also be linked to the type of treatment you choose. Prefrontal Involvement, Central Slowing, or Temporal Lobe ADHD as identified by the brain scan will each require a different approach and intervention. I will discuss this with treatment approaches in a later chapter, but **the first step is to ensure that you have a proper diagnosis**.

KEY IDEA FROM THIS STRATEGY

A *comprehensive assessment should include:

- complete review of possible medical factors that could be contributing to the symptoms;

- developmental and early learning history;

- test of focus and attention while completing a timed task in a lab setting (i.e., CPT);

- screening for Central Auditory Processing Disorder;

- Intelligence testing to identify potential gifted behavior and rule out some learning disabilities;

- Comprehensive achievement testing (i.e., WIAT);

- neuroimaging or brain scan reviewed by a neurologist and brain physiologist;

- comprehensive report with specific recommendations for home and school, or work and social for adults.

*You may be wondering if this is one big push to have you bring your child to our offices for assessment. Not so. I truly believe that, regardless of where you live, only a comprehensive assessment will do when the question of ADHD is at issue. Find a competent psychologist or clinic in your community that can do the tests I have outlined. Costs will vary. At our offices, at the writing of this book, we charge $2,750 for a child and $1,635 for an adult assessment with complete report, including the neurologist's evaluation. It's about the value of the service you receive. Parents tell me it's less than the cost of putting their child in hockey camp for the summer, so you decide what is most important. Most clinics such as ours also assist with filling out insurance and government program forms that may pay for all or part of these types of assessments.

STRATEGY 4
Understanding Complex ADHD

Complex ADHD refers to a diagnosis based on a comprehensive assessment process. It determines that two or more conditions, along with ADHD, exist that may impact learning. The isolated diagnosis of ADHD is very rare in our clinics. ADHD often co-exists with a specific learning disability, or Central Auditory Processing Disorder, Gifted Potential, and at times social skills deficits.

It is only possible to rule out Complex ADHD with a comprehensive assessment. Emotional factors are also often present, most commonly depression. For adolescents and adults, screening for self-medication using marijuana and other non-prescribed treatments. Excessive use of marijuana, for example, may contribute to fluctuations in focus and attention during the day, and that is more attributed to withdrawal or excessive use than to neurologically based ADHD.

What do these symptoms look like at home?

Children with Complex ADHD often appear to be gifted in many structured or stimulating environments. When things are going their way, when they are engaging in the tasks they find beneficial and enjoyable, the behavioral outcomes are very positive. We often see, however, that the ability to concentrate diminishes quickly over time, more so than non-ADHD children. The gifted part of ADHD often causes frustration and surprisingly negative self-esteem creation. Children and adults know that they are very good at doing certain tasks at certain times. What is frustrating is the aspect of ADHD that does not permit them to perform in such a fashion consistently over time. The great hockey player scoring three goals in one game can't do anything right the next time. The college or university student who gets 85 percent on one paper, gets 45 percent on the next, but believes they put in the same amount of work this time as last. Poor effort management is often the key factor minimizing consistent gifted behavior over time. Poor effort management refers to the disconnect between the effort demonstrated and that needed to complete a task effectively. Effort is poorly managed and understood by those of us with ADHD.

What can parents do with Complex ADHD?

Get to know your child's profile. What type of ADHD, how severe are the symptoms, what type of learning disability, and the specific gifted areas all need to be identified.

Celebrate success. Provide your child or teen with ample opportunity to practice what they are very good at, not just "remediation" for the things they don't do well.

Educate your child's teachers or educators. Help them understand, send them this book, or ask for a meeting to explain.

Make sure your child understands. If we as adults don't "get it," how can we expect the ten year old to understand? Explain the issue of learning style, how coaching and structure can help, and how the different types of ADHD can lead to different challenges.

Don't use the ADHD excuse. Find solutions, not excuses, for performance deficits.

Chart symptoms, progress, and successful strategies. The goal is to have a toolbox of successful strategies before entering college or university. While www.trackadhd.com can be helpful, use of www.goaltracker.ca (both free programs) can also help with this process.

Get good coaching. No two children are alike. Specific strategies for your child may differ from the next, especially if it is Complex ADHD. Coaching can help starting at about grade 4 and extending into adulthood.

What do symptoms look like in the classroom? An open letter to teachers.

Dear Teacher:

As a teacher, when you see a child in elementary school fidget at their seat, talk at the wrong times, have problems staying seated, appear disorganized, and at times show oppositional or defiant behavior, what would you think?

Remember to respect the power you have in the actual diagnosis of ADHD. If you think the child has ADHD, and you fill out a checklist as if this is true, then more than likely the child will receive this diagnosis and be placed on medication. You do know you were not trained in the diagnosis of ADHD, right?

These children appear to have ADHD, but if you dig a little deeper you will perhaps (in cases where this is true) see some problems in expressive language, or spelling, or writing. If you look really deeply, more than most, you will likely find areas of gifts or positive exceptional attributes. If this is so, make sure you start by explaining those to parents and doctors before becoming too focused on the ADHD symptoms. This will help those involved begin to search for the bigger picture. When you provide the child with an opportunity to engage in the areas that they are exceptionally gifted in, do they continue to have focus or distractibility problems?

I believe that the role of the teacher in this process is to provide expert opinion on the performance of the child in the classroom, during free-time play, and on the playground. Unbiased documentation is what is needed to assist in better understanding these children.

What can teachers do with Complex ADHD?

Teachers can:

- ✓ Provide ample opportunity for the child to demonstrate and practice their "gifts."

- ✓ Provide firm structure with ample opportunity for rewards.

- ✓ Provide a quiet place for the child to complete seat work.

- ✓ Plan for each of the areas identified. Specific strategies for the type of ADHD, learning disability, and gifted area.

- ✓ Assist the student in developing the toolbox of successful strategies to use in college or university. At a very early age, these children need to hear that they are going to make it, and that they will achieve their goals; we just need to find the path for them to get there.

- ✓ Be sensitive to the self-esteem issues associated with Complex ADHD. Praise is only effective if genuine and earned. Learning from failure, or even embracing failure, as part of the learning process needs to be emphasized.

- ✓ Work to identify what barriers are stopping this child from performing to their potential. What strategies will unlock this brilliance?

KEY IDEA FROM THIS STRATEGY

- Complex ADHD is a condition where ADHD exists along with one other diagnosed condition, including learning disability, central auditory processing, giftedness, or emotional problems. Different types of ADHD may also exist within one individual.

- A comprehensive assessment is needed to identify Complex ADHD.

- The treatment goal is to provide a toolbox of successful strategies that will enhance performance and help the student find their ADHD success.

STRATEGY 5
BUILD STRUCTURE

When I was told for the third time that I had central and right frontal slowing that was classic ADHD, it finally started to make sense. I was relieved to know that I wasn't "lazy" or "stupid" or without potential. Because of the mild nature of my ADHD, there would be days when I would look and perform like "normal" and other days much less so. On those days when I would fail, the comparison to my successful ones would cause me great pain and anxiety. I would ask myself, Why is it that yesterday I could do this and today I can't? What is wrong with me? Years of this kind of self-talk can lead to self-doubt, self-esteem issues, and in some cases depression. Getting an accurate diagnosis can be liberating and lead to a successful life plan. The diagnosis is the first step in finding your ADHD success.

The next step after your diagnosis is to **build predictable structure in your life**. I am often amazed at how successful athletes, students, business owners, and professionals with ADHD have been able to create their own "systems" and structure to ensure their success.

If you were to look at the military, it is a very structured environment where ADHD adults often thrive. As an enlisted soldier, you pretty much have your entire day planned from sun up to sun down. When you get up, when you brush your teeth, make your bed, automatically know what clothes to wear, how to act and behave. Every step is clearly defined.

If you choose to not follow this structure a very rapid and quick punishment is delivered. You would gradually learn to live within this structure created by others. Problems occur if this structure is suddenly taken away. There are many stories and discussions among military police of how for some soldiers living without these restrictions can be difficult. Suddenly presented with the option of total freedom, they often misbehave and engage in excessive alcohol consumption or disruptive behavior while on leave. I wonder what percentage of this group would have ADHD.

What do we mean by structure?

Structure is defined as **the limits self-imposed or imposed by others that define our actions throughout the day** (my definition here).

External structure is like the military, rules of conduct, and behavior that others put on you. With *internal structure*, the rules and expectations of "what to do" are self-created and self-directed. Children and adults with ADHD have some difficulty in moving from externally imposed rules and codes of conduct to internal ones at the same pace as those without ADHD.

While imposing "lockdown" structure can help a child or adult with ADHD, problems often occur when that external structure is removed. Parents, for example, will often quickly understand that when working with their child diagnosed with ADHD, **the more structure and rules with clear consequences and rewards the better**. But when that child leaves home to further their education, all external structure is removed and then there is a distinct need for internal, self-imposed structure, which requires significant skill on behalf of the child.

Building internal structures is the important goal of working with ADHD children and young adults so that they are able to impose the necessary expectations and rules for themselves.

If I am a 13-year-old boy with ADHD, part of my day will likely be very structured. The time I'm in school, I'm told when to get there, what to bring, how to behave, and what is expected of me on the athletic field. That external structure will be there until I graduate high school. But once at college or university, I am pretty much free to do what I want when I want each day. Of course, my parents are expecting me to attend class as expected, but no one takes attendance, no one yells at me or punishes me if I don't. I know on the first day of class as a college student what I need to do all year, when papers are due, when exams will be written, and the work that is needed to do well in each class because this information is provided. Unfortunately, no one provides a list of daily tasks that I need to do before those dates to accomplish success. I have one month before my first paper is due. Why start today?

Finding success with ADHD is about using the tools that work for you to break down the success you wish to achieve into daily tasks.

When I started looking at this concept, I used a whiteboard with yellow Post-it notes all over my office. At the top part of the whiteboard I would put my long-term goals, and underneath each day the tasks I needed to do that were linked with those goals. If my goal was to attain real estate success of having ten commercial properties within one year, then on a Monday I would write "search MLS for apartment buildings in Waterloo," for example.

For my health, I would have specific running programs that would tell me each day what to do. This structure, while awkward and not well-organized, helped me achieve my goals. I wondered, though, if an electronic version could do a better job. I tried to download various apps and other software, but without success.

Goaltracker.ca

I developed a web-based tool that you can find at www. goaltracker.ca to help with this task. The program is very simple. Using cloud-based technology, long-term goals are defined. Linked to each long-term goal are the daily tasks necessary to be successful. For example, a student may indicate that they wish to achieve honors standing in their area of concentrated study at university. Their long-term goal would be defined as "To achieve 80 percent in all of my English classes." Next, regular daily tasks, or one-time tasks, can be entered that will help the student achieve that goal. For example, from Monday to Thursday the task of "review notes from previous classes for one hour" will be added to the long-term goal. Each day from Monday to Thursday the student will be reminded through email or text message to complete that task. Once completed, a graph is presented to help show success. There is no limit to how many tasks can be linked to a long-term goal.

For those diagnosed with ADHD, the progression of structure from birth to adulthood is a gradual movement into independent adulthood. Having ADHD, however, requires that the structures be directly taught and gradually incorporated into the child's skill set.

Young children are provided structure to understand when it is best to set the alarm in the morning to get ready for school. Specific tasks are outlined on reminders, electronic or written, and posted schedules. **Children with ADHD gradually learn what structures are necessary to complete school assignments, home tasks or chores, and schedules of events with peers.** Over time, these structures are self-imposed in contrast to being demanded by parents.

For student athletes

Athletes diagnosed with ADHD, both young and experienced, need help in understanding what structure is necessary to achieve their potential.

A long-term goal for an athlete may be to make the high school track team twelve months from now. What structure is necessary for the athlete to achieve that goal? Using www.goaltracker.ca the athlete types in the long-term goal: "To make the track team next year in the 100 meter and 200 meter." Now the student puts in the different daily tasks necessary to complete that goal. Monday, Wednesday, and Friday are weight room and speed drill days. Tuesday and Thursday are conditioning days for the upper body. Tasks to achieve 75 percent grade average in school are also added because without that minimum grade, the student athlete cannot participate in extracurricular activities. So, Monday, Wednesday, and Friday would have one-hour tutoring. Tuesday and Thursday are "work ahead" days to spend on future projects or papers. Each day, one hour of homework is added to the task list. And so the list goes and grows according to each student and needs.

With the reminder function, the athlete is reminded each day through text message or email to do the tasks and then chart that they are completed. The structure of goaltracker.ca will provide the student with the self-imposed structure needed to be successful. The example of the athlete is just that—it works as well for any student with activities outside studies.

For adults

For adults with ADHD providing structure is usually centered on activities at work, with family, with friends, and home life. Structure for an adult is about creating the right tools and strategies for each individual task. Using goaltracker.ca, an adult with ADHD can set a long-term work goal to achieve to the next level within his work organization. This would result in a significant pay raise and increase in responsibility. Skills necessary for such a move up include being proficient in a number of human resources training modules offered by the company. The long-term goal entered is "To be named level 4 manager within twelve months." Tasks linked to that goal may include: "To complete one hour of the training module." This task is set for Monday, Wednesday, and Friday.

Another important task outlined to achieve the goal of moving up the next management level is to take a direct manager out to lunch monthly to connect and better understand the job demands. This is entered as a task to be done on a one-time basis, each month.

The job of building structure for ADHD is about moving from a point of parent or other imposed structure, to a system imposed by the individual with the diagnosis.

The goal is to have a self-imposed structure with tools that work prior to the last year of high school. For motivated adults with the proper coaching, achieving the desired structure could take from six to twelve months after receiving the diagnosis of ADHD.

If you choose to not use this software, a whiteboard and yellow Post-it notes will work as well. But you must refer to it daily. Www.goaltracker.ca is free for you to use. I still use it daily.

KEY IDEA FROM THIS STRATEGY

- Structure is about providing goals, tasks, rules and consequences to help achieve ADHD success.

- Over time, we move from external to internal or self-directed forms of structure.

- Online tools such as www.goaltracker.ca can help create this structure.

STRATEGY 6
SELF-TASK MATCHING

You are about to sit down to do some work, but are having a difficult time getting started. Your mind continues to wander, and to bring it back to the task at hand seems excruciatingly painful. You stare at the page you are supposed to be editing, but nothing is happening. Your brain feels like it is heavy, tired, and fuzzy. If you have ADHD and you have experienced this type of challenge, you know that you could easily rate your level of focus to be a 10 out of 10, 0 reflecting laser-like focus and 10 a total inability to concentrate. If you try to do the work at level 10 (no concentration whatsoever), you will fail.

If you don't have ADHD but are trying to better understand a child or adult partner, think to a time when you were required to take part in all-day training at work, in a conference room, reading slides and handouts. At about 2 in the afternoon, you likely had a difficult time focusing on the mundane material. **Having untreated ADHD is like living your life at the end of a training day. It is very boring, with occasional moments of interest or energy.** It actually hurts to concentrate on most tasks, and it may seem at times for the person with ADHD that the brain has simply run out of gas.

If my level of focus is an 8 (very poor ability to concentrate) and I am working on a task that requires at least a 4 (rather focused) so I can accomplish it successfully in a reasonable period of time, then I will be frustrated if I attempt to do the task. The level of focus for someone with ADHD may fluctuate throughout the day. An hour ago I was about a 3, but now due to the fatigue of the day, lack of snack, and wearing off of caffeine in coffee, it's an 8. If I don't understand this problem, I will likely start to turn the blame inward, as voiced by others.

"Henry, I don't understand. Yesterday you were able to do your work at such a high level and today you just sit there. You seem lazy and unmotivated today. Is something wrong at home?" (Many of my teachers and professors would search for an answer.)

I start to also wonder: I did a pretty good job yesterday, so something is wrong with me. I'm not a very good student and I'm not very good at school. Maybe I'm lazy.

When I get home I have to do the work I couldn't do at school for homework. But now I'm a 10 (total lack of focus), so while my parents stand over me for two hours, I do manage to complete the work, but it looks horrible. My parents are screaming and upset, I'm feeling very stupid, and so it goes on and on each day and each night. Eventually, I find very neat ways to stop the madness. I refuse to do the work. I forget my books at school. I get into trouble in the classroom each time I start to wander, so I go down to the principal's office and answer phones. Self-esteem then becomes the main issue and block for me to achieve to my potential. Later you will learn more of why this is a significant problem, but for now let's go back to the self-monitoring challenge.

Self-monitoring

The first step in teaching self-monitoring is to get very good at understanding how focused you might be at any one time. Right now, as you read this, rate yourself on a scale from 0 (very focused) to 10 (totally out to lunch, fuzzy thinking, unable to focus on anything except very stimulating tasks, such as a video game). You may need to better explain how your level of focus "feels" to others and have them rate you.

Over time, you need to get very good at self-monitoring.

You can use two software tools I have developed to learn self-monitoring and charting. At www.trackadhd.com you can track your level of focus on an ongoing basis.

In www.goaltracker.ca you are asked to track your level of focus when you complete certain tasks. You are also asked to rate the level of focus required to complete each task successfully. This is our next step.

Task monitoring

In your work or school day you have many demands placed upon your time. You have to respond to emails and correspondence, take notes, and pay attention to the teacher. You may have to approve invoices or staff hours. You may have to edit written work or conduct research on the Internet, or write an in-class essay. For each of your daily tasks you need to provide a rating as to the highest number (worst focus) you can have to do the task at an exceptional level. For me, to edit any work, or re-read something that I have written, requires a level 3 for me to successfully accomplish the task. Researching a topic on the Internet can be done effectively even if I am at a level 10 (absolutely no focus) because of the ever-changing and rewarding task of surfing the Internet and doing research.

Now here is the problem. If you get very good at self-monitoring, and then can successfully rate all tasks you have to do in your world, what do you do if the numbers don't match?

If I need to sit down quietly and edit work that is due tomorrow and I am at a level 6, I have a number of choices. The work requires a level 3 or less to do it properly. I can put the work aside and wait it out till I will be a 3 or less; in my case, this is usually at 6 or 7 in the morning after my first coffee. I can do some aerobic exercise, which usually brings me into focus by two to three points. The problem is that I already did that this morning. I can try to plug through the work even though I am not focused, which will lead to frustration, use of excessive time, and a poor work product.

My choice is to do the work tomorrow morning after my first coffee in time for the deadline.

Now let's say I'm a level 3 and I have a choice of tasks to complete. I know I have that paper to edit for work, but I really want to surf the Internet and do some research on a new project. I can surf the Internet when my level of focus and concentration is up to a 9/10. If I do the research on the web when I am at a level 3 (excellent focus and concentration), then I have wasted that opportunity. I should have chosen to edit the work because that was the most efficient use of my time at this moment.

Task and self-monitoring is necessary for ADHD success because of the wide fluctuations in the ability to focus and concentrate within short periods of time.

Without ADHD your level of focus would likely range from 1-4 or 5 depending on your intake of food and sleep the night before. With ADHD that range can be from 1-10 changing quickly based on environmental demands and personal characteristics. It is the difference between your level of focus and the level needed to complete a task effectively that often leads to frustration, anger, and poor self-esteem

---

Matching your level of focus with the tasks at hand is one of the key skills you will need to learn to achieve ADHD success.

What level of focus is required for each task?

This is an important question and a difficult one if you have never thought of this concept. A good rule of thumb is a level 1-3 is needed if the task requires intense concentration or is considered very "boring" to you.

A level of 4-6 is needed for tasks that allow for the interaction with others, fairly interesting topics for brief bursts of time. Attending a 30-minute meeting on a topic you are particularly interested in may represent such a task.

Finally, those tasks that you find extremely motivating and interesting, with constant changing feedback, could likely be completed successfully at a 7-10 level of focus and concentration. Surfing the Internet, playing a video game with friends, brainstorming new ideas at work, are some examples. You will need to work at the self-task matching exercise to begin to understand what tasks are best done at certain times for you personally.

It takes a great deal of energy to remember, think, and focus. It's important not to confuse brain fatigue with focus and concentration levels. I have learned over time that certain foods and a certain diet, with exercise, will maximize my ability to concentrate and focus for greater periods of time. I have also learned that these foods are commonly found around us: yogurt, fruit, protein, and not much sugar. Sugar seems to give me a sudden burst of energy, but then the crash is strongly felt and brings me to a level 8-10 on the focus and concentration scale. What makes sense for you?

You too will learn what activities, foods, or techniques will help you maximize your ability to focus. Start a food journal and jot down how you feel after you eat something. You may start to find a pattern, both good and bad.

What are you supposed to do if you are faced with a task that requires a level 3 (very focused), but you are at a level 7 (very poor concentration)?

My answer to this is always the same: If you have time to do activities that have proven to increase your level of focus, such as 30 minutes of cardio or walking, do it. If you can stop and do some deep breathing or mental imagery that may get you to a level 5 or 6 (which, while not optimal, will help you get through the task) then do that

---

It is the ineffective match between the task and your level of concentration at the time that is the problem—it is not because you are lazy or don't care.

Your level of focus is simply not matching the task. Finding your ADHD success is about learning the skill of self-task matching.

You can start working with children as young as 6 or 7 on this skill. Don't expect your child to fully master this skill until more senior elementary grades. By starting early, however, children begin to learn the concept and preserve their important self-esteem, a factor that is extremely valuable to finding ADHD success.

You can develop a simple paper chart to track the level of focus you are experiencing throughout the day. This will help get you "tuned in" to this strategy.

Next, chart your level of focus just before you try to do a specific task. Rate yourself and then rate the level you feel you need to do the task effectively. You want to be within 2 scale points of what the task needs. If the task requires a 4 and you are at a level 1, then you should pick a task that requires more focus because you are very focused at this time. You can do the task if you need to, but don't waste this valuable time on something that you can do easily.

If you are at a level 6 (not the greatest focus) and the task requires a 2 (requires a great deal of focus), then try to improve your level of focus or delay completing the task until you have a better match.

The software tool www.goaltracker.ca has a built-in system to help you with this self-task strategy. It requires you to indicate the level of focus needed to complete a given task. When you chart your completion of the task, it asks you to rate your level of focus when you did the task. It then provides a graph of the differences between these two scores over time. Goaltracker.ca is an excellent tool to help you, or your child, master the self-task strategy.

KEY IDEA FROM THIS STRATEGY

- Self-task matching is an important skill to learn to find your ADHD success.

- Children should start in elementary school by self-rating their focus on a scale of 1 (very focused) to 10 (totally unable to focus).

- Learning to identify what level of focus is necessary to complete a task successfully is the next step.

- Build a toolbox of activities or foods that may help you increase your level of focus when you absolutely must do a certain task, but have a bit of time to use a strategy.

- If you have the time, delay doing a task until your level of focus equals that which is required.

- You can use simple pencil or paper to begin to build this skill, or software tools such as www.goaltracker.ca developed specifically for this task.

STRATEGY 7
BUILD SELF-ESTEEM

Self-esteem is about the thoughts and feelings we have about our competence as a person. It is what we say to our self about our self:

> ➤ "I am strong, powerful, and in control."
> ➤ "I am confident in my abilities on the athletic field."
> ➤ "I am a great writer."

Our self-esteem is developed or blocked by our own thoughts and beliefs and our interactions with the world, including those important adults around us, such as parents, teachers, or coaches. A strong positive self-esteem drives children to be inquisitive, with little fear of failure. In the classroom, it means taking chances with ideas, challenging those in authority when a cause is identified, and achieving greatness. This strong self-esteem is a vital component to ADHD success.

With ADHD, self-esteem takes a beating due to the strong differences in performance from day to day, and even moment to moment.

These differences make others in power, such as teachers or parents, wonder about your abilities overall, why your attitude and work ethic fluctuate so much. They question your character, and soon statements such as "You are lazy," "You don't seem to want to do the work needed to be a success," "If you could do this yesterday why can't you do it today?" "You have a bad attitude," are internalized and become part of a negative or poor self-esteem. Homework often attempted when mental and cognitive fatigue is at their highest (in the evening), reinforces these negative beliefs. It takes sixty minutes to do ten minutes of "real work." Very soon the young child with ADHD begins to internalize these negative experiences and statements, which then lead to failure.

When working on my master's degree, I researched the self-esteem of high school dropouts compared to those who intended to graduate. I found that those who didn't complete school often didn't do so because they had few social supports, or advocates, encouraging them along the way. Dropping out of school had nothing to do with intelligence, learning ability, self-esteem or academic skill. Some 30 percent or more of high-school dropouts at that time were designated as gifted. I wonder how many high-school dropouts today have ADHD or gifted ADHD?

Successful adults know that they can't be good at everything and early in life stop trying to do that. As adults we are fine with that. We have strong self-esteems in those very specific areas that we excel. Children, however, have more of a global self-esteem that carries over into other areas of their lives. If at recess they aren't picked to be on a sports team, a 7-year-old will rarely say, "I'm just not very good at soccer and that's okay because I'm great at chess." Rather, the child will likely use that experience to state to other adults, "I'm just not very popular at recess; the other kids won't pick me for teams. I'm not very good at soccer, and I'm just not very good at anything."

How do we develop self-esteem?

Let's look at how you developed self-esteem as a child. Much has been said about unconditional love and acceptance. It's about being accepted for who you are and the ability of your parents to separate your behavior from who you are as a person. The job of parents is to provide children with a safe and secure environment from which to explore their world. As a baby, you started to crawl, exploring the house (when allowed) on all fours. Your parents were there should you stub your toe, to reassure you, and to encourage you to continue to take these risks in moving away from them.

If they didn't let you crawl, and kept you in their lap because of fear you would fall again, then how would you ever move on to explore the house, the yard, the neighborhood, the school, and so on? So while they encouraged you to move away from them, to be independent, they did it as you developed the skills and maturity to handle that freedom. You became more confident as you progressed, often rewarded by your parents for taking those steps and accomplishments. Your self-esteem was built up over time and by one successful experience after another.

If you have ADHD, however, the transition and movement to build self-esteem may have been hampered. Depending on your activity levels as a child, you may have been very difficult to handle, to take out in public, to go to restaurants with, and so on. While it may have been your behavior that was causing the problems, you likely very quickly began to internalize those negatives or punishments as indications that there was something wrong with you, that you were somewhat deficient and not capable.

Starting school would prove to be very challenging as well. Even if diagnosed with Inattentive Type-ADHD, your self-esteem would be challenged by the fluctuations in performance. Often teachers and parents point to poor attitude, effort, or intentionally doing poorly. The word "lazy" often appears. These statements do little to enhance self-esteem. Remember, most don't understand the self-task matching skills you just read about in the previous chapter that were the true reasons for your fluctuations in performance. Impulsivity on the playground and oppositional behavior not understood by educators also contributes to negative experiences.

So how do we fix this?

Strong, positive self-esteem is like an internal rock of stability that is the base from which all risk-taking and life exploring will occur. This rock gives us the strength to try new things, take chances and calculated risks. Failing is part of progress.

A great baseball player doesn't get a hit seven out of ten times that they try. Outstanding sales professionals will tell you that if they make ten phone calls they will get three meetings that will result in one sale. Ninety percent of the time they will not be successful. Google understands that 95 percent of the time a new product or service they create will fail, but they also realize that the 5 percent that make it are game changers. Think of the confidence necessary to fail nine out of ten times when we try something new? It is the strong rock or self-esteem that helps protect us during these times of failure.

The first step in building strong positive self-esteem is to fix the rock. Building a strong sense of confidence, security, and positive self-talk about success is necessary. Focusing on success and learning from failure is a way of thinking that will help. Psychologists talk about cognitive behavioral "work" (CBT), which is learning to change the way we think of our experiences in the world.

For example, the child who states "I didn't get picked for soccer at recess, I have no friends, I am not good at anything" is using a form of catastrophic thinking that erodes self-esteem. CBT would work to help the child understand that one experience on the soccer field is not reflective of the whole person. Quickly, other more positive experiences with peers are discussed to help the child understand that global negative statements aren't true.

Learning to think differently about negative life experiences is a key training tool to build positive self-esteem.

Understanding your ADHD diagnosis is the next step in building self-esteem

Knowing the type of your ADHD, how it impacts your learning and behavior is important.

If something isn't working out well, look at the structure in your environment or self-task focus match as discussed in our earlier chapters, as the first answer to explain what is going on. Don't quickly resort to personal attacks such as "what is wrong with me" or "I am so lazy today" or other self-defeating statements. Do the tasks and strategies to create the structure needed or self-task focus match problem.

If some of your childhood negative experience is getting in the way of moving forward you may need the help of a trained professional or coach to move you forward. My experience is that the majority of parents do the best that they can in raising their children. Most make mistakes (and we all do) while trying to help their children. A small group don't get it and have no skills to parent. It's no one's fault: they just don't have what it takes to be a mom or dad. It's also not their fault if they didn't fully understand your ADHD.

Helping you move beyond the negative feelings you have about these childhood experiences is often a focus of this therapy. Once you are liberated from these self-defeating statements and thoughts you will be ready to achieve ADHD success.

Researchers tell us that it can take from ten to twenty years of practice and hard work to be good at any one thing. It takes a great positive self-esteem to buffer you while you experience the failures of twenty years of trying. Music, painting, engineering, writing, building, designing—you name it and the evidence is clear: great work is made, not born.

Say no to build self-esteem

Say no more often. Let's say that you are asked to help a neighbor paint their garage. You aren't very good at painting, don't like doing it, and inevitably make all kinds of mistakes when you try. Being able to paint a house or garage is not important to you. As a result, you have the confidence to say thank you for the offer, but I won't be helping you paint the garage. Painting isn't something I do.

Now your friend may look at you and wonder what this means. Perhaps you can help in other ways—prepare a lunch, bring over some beverages, cut her grass while she is painting, or help out in some other way. Or just say no. Saying no to others more often will help build your self-esteem.

KEY IDEA FROM THIS STRATEGY

- ADHD self-esteem takes a beating due to many negative childhood experiences. Fluctuations in performance (great one day, horrible the next) lead to questions of character, attitude, and effort, which all contribute to negative self-esteem.

- Positive self-esteem is the rock or internal security needed to find ADHD success.

- Understanding the ADHD diagnosis, finding the right structure, and understanding the self-task focus match are helpful strategies.

- Cognitive behavioral therapy is a helpful therapeutic technique to change the way you think about your life experience.

- Strong self-esteem is needed to buffer you from the failures during the twenty years of practice it takes to be great at any one thing.

- Saying no more often will help you build your self-esteem.

STRATEGY 8
GETTING THE RIGHT TREATMENT

So far you have learned strategies that you can use to help you or your child fit into different systems or environments. These strategies will help you find ADHD success. But what should you do if you or your child have such significant attention, concentration, or focus problems that you cannot benefit from this work? What if your child can't sit still long enough to learn the self-task focus strategy?

As discussed, the symptoms you are seeing are due to brain deregulation. We know of only two ways to change the ADHD brain. One method is to take medications; the other is to train with EEG biofeedback.

Taking medication

A variety of medications are available for children and adults to help control the symptoms of ADHD. There are also a number of excellent resources available to help you research the side effects and profiles of each. One resource is this website: www.nlm.nih.gov/medlineplus/druginformation.html.

Medications are designed to reduce the symptoms of being unable to pay attention, concentrate, or focus; they are not designed to replace the need to learn strategies to find ADHD success.

Used properly, medications will improve your focus and concentration so that you will be more likely to learn the strategies we have discussed.

I am often asked in my practice if a child or adult should or should not be placed on medication. This decision is one that should be made by considering the severity of the ADHD symptoms, the wishes of the parents and child, and medical opinions. The wishes of the custodial parents override any other opinions or wishes.

Teachers and principals cannot insist that medication be a prerequisite to being allowed entry to school. That is illegal in most jurisdictions.

If you choose medications

Methylphenidate, amphetamines, atomoxetine, guanfacine, clonidine, and some antidepressants may be prescribed by your physician. Health care providers not providing accurate information about these and other medications is one of the main reasons that medication is not taken regularly, is discontinued, or is used improperly. For this reason, I have developed another free tool for you to use at www.trackadhd.com.

This site allows you to enter ratings for concentration, focus, and other symptoms, and then print out a graph when you see your doctor for that follow-up visit. It also allows you to ask others to provide charting (without seeing your data or personal information), such as classroom teachers, so that their observations will also be noted. By reviewing your charts and graphs, your doctor will get a better idea of how you are progressing over time, and thus make minor adjustments in your dosage to maximize your performance and minimize any side effects.

Although ADHD is a life-long condition, many diagnosed will stop taking their medication prematurely. Often this is because they believe they don't need the medication because they no longer have symptoms. Unfortunately, once the medication is no longer present in their systems, the problems will reappear. Others have reported that they stop taking medication because of cost, side effects, or that they forget to take it consistently. All of these reasons can be managed by providing the proper structure necessary. Accurate, timely feedback to your physician with relevant data, combined with the input of others, is the key to making sure that you maximize the benefits of medication.

Neurofeedback training

The theory of neurofeedback training is based on the belief that localized parts of the brain are deregulated and cause the presenting problems of ADHD. Dr. Daniel Amen, a widely accepted researcher in the field, has discovered six different types of ADHD based on the localized area where that deregulation occurs. Other researchers have reported that individuals with temporal lobe ADHD, for example, are more prone to bouts of anger, negative self-esteem, and often central auditory processing problems, while those with more central "slowing" have difficulty getting started with tasks and organizational skills. According to this theory, medications and neurofeedback treatment should be based on the brain image, which helps determine the type of ADHD and the exact location of the problem.

Neurofeedback has been defined as a type of biofeedback that uses electroencephalography to provide a signal that can be used by a person to receive feedback regarding brain activity. The feedback is often provided back to the user in the form of sound or some other form of feedback.

As an example, let's assume that you have had a complete assessment and the brain scan suggests right prefrontal slowing. A specific treatment schedule is suggested and you agree to use neurofeedback to help with the symptoms. A small sensor is placed on your scalp in the spot that has been shown to be deregulated, and ground sensors are placed on your ears. The sensors listen to or pick up electrical activity from your scalp; they do not put anything into your brain. Just as a heart rate monitor "listens" to your heart, the EEG sensor "listens" to your brain.

Let's assume that the assessment showed us that in this specific part of your brain you are not sending out enough low beta waves, those waves necessary for focused concentration. The software is set so that each time that part of your brain sends out the correct level of beta you are rewarded by scoring points or are allowed to watch a movie. At first, this happens randomly as you have no way to manipulate this fact. Over time, however, you begin to "get it" and learn what state your brain needs to be in to score points and win the video game.

Unlike medication, the changes noted by engaging in neurofeedback remain after treatment is completed, which is a significant benefit and advantage. On the negative side, neurofeedback is often accomplished with one or two visits per week over many months; this can take a great deal of time. Some twenty to fifty visits (or more, even) are often required to see significant changes in ADHD symptoms. For about 15-20 percent of cases, this treatment has not been effective.

There are skeptics who question the research that has been conducted on the benefits of neurofeedback. However, my experience has been very positive. I have undergone over thirty neurofeedback treatments and can honestly say it has had a significant impact on my ability to focus, concentrate, and get work accomplished. You will read in the final chapter how my son Joshua also used neurofeedback to improve his attention and concentration skills. You can find further resources, articles, and videos describing neurofeedback training for ADHD at our practice web site www.drsvec.com.

KEY IDEA FROM THIS STRATEGY

- Medication can be an effective tool to help manage the symptoms of ADHD. Key to this is to make sure you have a system that allows you to keep track of the changes in symptoms and report those to your doctor on a regular basis.

- Neurofeedback can be of benefit to help reduce ADHD symptoms by targeting specific localized areas of the brain that show deregulation with a brain scan.

- Neurofeedback requires ongoing monitoring of symptom changes, as with medication.

- Neurofeedback can take months of work before benefits are realized. 15-20 percent of people with ADHD do not seem to improve with this technique. However, once symptoms do improve, these changes remain once treatment is completed (from twenty to fifty visits).

STRATEGY 9
FIGHT DEPRESSION

More than 80 percent of adults with ADHD report that they also experience depression or depressive feelings on a regular basis. Is this because the neurology or brain abnormalities that cause ADHD also cause depression? Or could it be that the negative life events associated with ADHD lead to depression? Let us first look at the different theories of how and why we become depressed and see what may fit.

Loss

All of us experience depression or depressive feelings when we lose something of significance (like a job) or someone close to us. You've likely watched that National Geographic special about the method of grieving that elephants go through when they lose a partner. Grieving is a natural process, as is the sadness that goes along with it.

ADHD may have caused you to lose many things: a job, relationship, friends or peers at school, or the loss of the dream of success that you once had. Experiencing loss may be one of the most significant factors contributing to depression and ADHD.

You're not having much fun

Believe it or not, researchers some years ago suggested that we get depressed when our days aren't a lot of fun, and we aren't doing the things that give us joy. As a result, in the late 1970s many hospitals treating depressed patients established "Pleasant Effect Schedules," which was a daily schedule of having fun. Not surprisingly, patients exposed to everything from funny movies to great experiences, felt lifted and were no longer as depressed. But while having fun all day may lift a mild or moderate depressed mood, does a lack of that necessarily contribute to depression? The jury is still out on this theory.

Loss of control

Put any healthy human or animal in a situation where they lack control over their environment and depression gradually sets in. Early experiments were conducted with animals in laboratories where it was learned that healthy dogs develop depression rather quickly once total control is taken away.

Negative experiences for humans tend to take away our control. Children and adults with ADHD quickly learn that they have little control over their environments when they do not comply with what is asked of them by school teachers or supervisors in a work setting. All of those creative activities, or ideas, are out of reach. Eventually, when faced with compliance or punishment, the perception or belief is that control has been taken away.

However, even more powerful with ADHD, is the self-limiting behaviors that occur based on consistent negative feedback and failure over time. As a child or adult with ADHD you eventually stop trying, and begin to believe that you have no control over anything in your environment, which then leads to a type of reactive depression. If not treated, this depression can become debilitating.

The Loss of Control Theory has lead to the development of cognitive behavioral treatment that attacks this belief system. A simple way to describe it is that Cognitive Behavioral Therapy (CBT) changes the way we think about things that happen to us at any given time. It is a powerful tool to fight depression that often comes with ADHD.

Some rules of Cognitive Behavioral Therapy

There are some things in life that you can't control

Trying to control what we can't leads to frustration, anger, and finally depression. We have no ability to control the majority of events that occur around us. If you accept this, then why waste time trying to change the things you cannot change? In relationships, believe what you see. You cannot change someone who doesn't want to change. Accept it and focus your valuable time and energy on those aspects of your life that you can control.

You did the best you could with what you knew at the time

We all make mistakes—some more hurtful and harmful than others. You have made decisions in the past based on what you knew or felt at the time. Looking back now, it may not seem like the best solution or path or decision, but at the time you felt it was the correct path. Hopefully, you have learned from each of those experiences, and you must, therefore, accept that you did the best you could with what you knew at that time. Going back and hammering away at your self-esteem is not helpful, nor can it change what has happened in the past.

There are many different answers to a problem; look at all of them

With ADHD, we often see what is called a rigid or fixed way to look at a problem or solution. Some therapists wonder if this personality trait is common among those of us with ADHD.

Let's assume that we are sitting across the table from one another and a Kleenex box is between us. My side of the box has a picture of a hockey player on it, your side a picture of a figure skater. I try to explain to you that I have a hockey player on the box, but you can only see the figure skater; you are unable to see my side of the story, as it were. You can't let your opinion go for even a minute or two to really see my side of that box.

This is what often occurs with ADHD. The rigid fixed way of thinking gets in the way of learning the various options and solutions that are available in different situations. Time and practice will help, but this is a difficult trait to overcome. It often leads to anger and depression because an absolute way of thinking when interacting with authority figures always leaves the individual with ADHD feeling as if they have lost. Understanding that there are different solutions that may have a better outcome is a challenge and a key to overcoming ADHD depression.

While you often can't control events that happen, you can control your reactions to them

> ➢ A teacher tells you that your work is not acceptable.

> ➢ A manager at works calls you into her office to complain about your lack of participation in a recent staff meeting.

> ➢ Your spouse wonders why you are looking disinterested when she talks with you.

These events happen; they are not within your control once they have occurred, so the question is what can you do about it? In the first example, you can argue, be disrespectful, fight with them, or have your parents fight with the teacher. Not likely a fruitful reaction on your part if you want to get a good grade in that class. You may not care, choose to be your own person and not take it anymore. That is fine, if that is your thought-out choice. While you are not often responsible for the things that happen to and around you, you are responsible for how you react to them. You have the power and opportunity to control that.

Life is not fair (not necessarily a CBT solution, but one needed to remember with ADHD)

Some years ago, I was working with a child who had gotten into trouble at recess. While standing in line after the bell, he turned around and punched the boy standing right beside him. When asked, he indicated it wasn't his fault and he did nothing wrong. The boy was diagnosed with ADHD. Further prodding revealed that just before the punch, the victim had bumped into the boy with ADHD. "He made me do it; if he hadn't bumped into me I wouldn't have had to punch him."

Getting caught for punching the boy didn't seem fair to my client. He was just getting "caught." It is true that children with ADHD are more likely to get "caught" breaking rules at recess. We are starting to wonder if it is because they actually engage in more negative behavior, or if teachers are just watching them because of their diagnosis. Perhaps, and more likely, they aren't as sophisticated at breaking the rules, show impulse at the wrong time, and therefore get easily found out (like punching a student while standing in line after the bell with the teacher watching). Regardless, life is not fair. Once caught, the question is what should the child do? Yes, this is not fair; life is not fair. Get over it and learn to deal with it. They are all life lessons.

Bad things happen to good people

This is a fact. We hear this every day. The child in school is killed crossing the street. The super mom, hit by a drunk driver and killed instantly. Great, inspiring, honest people taken from us in an instant. Many years ago I was working to help a community work through a very horrible tragedy. At the end of a long and challenging day, I found myself sitting with a group of professionals, including the local clergy, who were also working very hard to help the community. I asked him how he dealt with, or internalized, the fact that a bad thing had just happened to a good group of people.

He looked at me and said, "At funerals, I'm supposed to say that they are in a better place, we're called to a higher need for service and so on. Frankly, Henry, I don't get it. I never have. It is not fair, not right, not just. Bad things just happen to good people." Some months later I learned that he had left the priesthood and gotten married. Sometimes good things happen to good people.

Depression saps us of our energy to enjoy life. At the extreme, it may start us down the path of suicidal thinking or planning. If depression is something you are experiencing, seek out the help of your health care provider immediately. As depression becomes more extreme, we lose the ability to engage in those activities such as exercise or socializing with others, tasks that can help us move out of depression naturally. Help from a psychologist can help you fight the pain of depression.

KEY IDEA FROM THIS STRATEGY

- ADHD and depression seem to go together; we just don't know why. Is it brain deregulation or negative life experiences that cause this depression?

- Cognitive Behavior Therapy (CBT) is often the treatment of choice for depression.

- CBT and other research help us understand the rules of thinking that can keep us healthy when faced with negative situations.

- Exercise and CBT, when combined, can help you find your ADHD success.

- If you or your child is experiencing depression that is impacting your daily life, or if there are any suicidal thoughts or actions, seek out help with your health care provider, physician, or psychologist immediately.

STRATEGY 10
BUILDING SOCIAL-EMOTIONAL INTELLIGENCE

There are many different ways to get to an outcome that you want when you are talking or interacting with others. Often with ADHD, it is the first response or impulse that gets us into trouble.

Let's say you are talking with your boss and she makes a condescending comment. You feel the anger swell up inside you and within seconds you want to lash out at her. You tell her she needs to get a real job and perhaps try living in your shoes for a day before she starts spouting off about something she knows nothing about.

Someone with a high social-emotional IQ would have taken a moment to gather their wits and let the emotions pass. The next thought would be, "What do I need to get from this conversation to achieve my goal?" You want to be neutral in this situation because you want to show strength and turn the negative into a positive. Saying something like, "I understand your point. I need to be more cautious when entering information into the database," will send the right message to your boss.

My definition of an extremely high social-emotional IQ is operating in the world with careful thought and restraint, and remembering to respond in a manner that is consistent with your goals and objectives. It is about taking a path that is best to achieve those goals. Emotion is rarely helpful unless you can channel it to create your desired outcome.

Another way to understand how to develop these areas of your life is to think of a non-assertive, assertive, and aggressive response to a problem. You are on the road traveling to a part of the country you will likely never see again. You order breakfast at the hotel because you don't want to look for it elsewhere. When the food arrives, you notice that the eggs aren't cooked as you had asked, the bacon is greasy and undercooked, and the toast is burnt. What should you do?

You pause for a moment, let your emotions work through, and then focus on what you would like as an outcome. You'd like your breakfast as you ordered it, without any cook "saliva" or other "treats" in it because kitchen staff were upset you sent it back. You decide you will call over the waitress and ask her what to do. As she arrives, you state, "I am sorry, but did I get someone else's breakfast? I had ordered bacon well done with whole wheat toast. Should I order again or try to work through this here?"

Now you can decide your next step based on how your waiter responds. If it is in a helpful, supportive manner, you may agree to send it back and get another try at it. Most of the time, you could just work through the meal (it is a $3.99 special) as best you can and leave.

By choosing this path you have made a choice based on a well-thought out plan, not emotions. With ADHD, emotion, including anger and hurt feelings, often drives us to engage in behavior that is rarely helpful. You need to develop a set of skills from the non-assertive to the assertive. There will be times that you will have to fight for what you believe is the right solution.

Non-assertive behavior is best defined as "doing nothing" and being very quiet as a strategy.

Assertive behavior is standing up for your rights without infringing upon the rights of others.

Instrumental aggression is assertiveness times ten. When using this skill you appear to be angry, or if need be aggressive, when in fact it is a well-controlled strategy to achieve your desired end result.

Many years ago I was walking the loading docks of a produce shipping market when I heard a number of different voices yelling rather loudly about the quality of the fruit. They were making negative comments on the grade, freshness, and taste. Back and forth it went rather loudly for a few more minutes. A deal was agreed upon by both parties, a handshake and a smile, and on to the next challenge. In buying produce in the 1980s at this market, being instrumentally aggressive was part of the culture and expectation to get a better price on a product. This wouldn't work in most settings, like trying to get a better price on a pair of shoes, but it did work in the produce business.

There are also times, hopefully rarely, when you may have to use instrumental aggression to litigate someone or use legal process to draw the line in the sand. Going to court, while expensive, is the only legal way to smash someone in the mouth for breaking rules, betraying your trust, trying to steal from you, or hurting your family.

When ADHD robs us of our self-esteem it becomes difficult to use assertive or instrumental aggression to achieve a goal. Part of this comes from believing that you don't deserve a better response, or you may lack confidence in your position. Years of failure, or being told you just aren't doing as well as you can, slowly erodes your confidence.

In the previous chapter I discussed how saying no can be the first step to building your self-esteem. It comes from within, where you feel strong and confident enough to say no to whatever is being asked of you. Saying no is an assertiveness strategy.

Just recently I was asked to play at a charity golf tournament. My wife and I support a number of charities and this was not one of them. I hate playing golf. It takes hours, usually kills a day, and isn't something I want to do. When asked, I responded honestly: "No, thank you. I don't golf." When pressed about why I had golfed in the past, I indicated that just recently I realized that I didn't like golfing and that was that. End of story. Now the look on the individual's face was interesting. In the past I would have given an excuse, or agreed to go and been miserable all day. Being assertive is standing up for what you believe in, but it starts with being true to yourself.

Developing strong and high emotional and social intelligence can take many years. With ADHD, it will likely take some years greater than those who don't have ADHD. The point is to continue moving forward working on the right things, making sure you have your long- and short-term goals in mind.

Cautionary note about using assertive or instrumentally aggressive strategies

Today, we are often inundated with the idea that we all will need to join hands and cooperate on most endeavors. Children are taught at an early age to be cooperative, to be like the others, and to not try to win at all costs. The problem is that once they all graduate, it does become a very competitive world where at times there are winners and losers.

If you display assertiveness to someone who isn't used to hearing the word no, you may be considered aggressive. That is why you need to review your strategy ahead of time and in consultation with a coach, mentor, or someone you trust to give you honest feedback; this is very important. This problem seems to be getting much worse as more and more children are being raised in an entitled environment; they just can't understand why in the adult world things don't always go their way.

When you start working on developing and improving your social-emotional intelligence you need to review your strategies and performance after each situation. Learn from this process and always ask yourself if your strategy was the best to help you achieve your goals.

KEY IDEA FROM THIS STRATEGY

- Social-emotional intelligence is about using the right strategy, without emotion, to get the outcome you want and need. This could include non-assertive, assertive, and instrumentally aggressive strategies.

- It can take many years of working with a coach or mentor to perfect this scale. Children need to learn the concepts very early and practice them with the long-term goal or outcome in mind.

- Responding too quickly or impulsively is often the reason those with ADHD have problems with their emotional IQ.

STRATEGY 11
LEARNING HOW TO ADVOCATE

I love this topic. I love fighting for something I believe in. As a teacher working with children who were living on the street, I would often fight with the schools for suspending or expelling them. I believed the main reason wasn't based on achievement or intelligence, but that these kids didn't have someone standing up for their rights.

There are three types of advocacy.

1. **Positive Advocacy** is where you fight for something and the people you are fighting against appreciate your efforts. Let's say you find that a certain product can be created in a more environmentally friendly way, so you present the idea to your supervisor at work. She agrees to "send it up the channel" because it will not only benefit the environment, but improve profit margins.

2. **Neutral Advocacy** is where you are fighting for a cause or issue and the other side doesn't feel good about that, but they are not upset with you for doing so. An example could be fighting a traffic ticket in court. The policeman knows that this happens on occasion and that it is your right. He would rather

have you not fight the ticket, but he has no feelings for you doing so, nor does the court. It is your right.

3. **Negative Advocacy** is where you are fighting for a cause and it causes negative feelings from the other side. My example of fighting for school dropouts is a negative advocacy strategy.

Most of us want to be liked by those around us, those we work with, and those that educate our children. You must remember that if you use a negative advocacy strategy at your child's school you aren't there all day to monitor how your child is treated. Your child must be able to advocate for themselves as well, or further damage will occur.

Having ADHD means you will have to use all three types of advocacy at some point to help you find your ADHD success.

If your child requires a certain type of structure and modifications to their educational program to be successful in school, you will have to fight for that. Start with positive strategies, of course, but you will likely have to resort to negative advocacy to make sure the schools listen. Eventually, your child will need to learn self-advocacy by the time they leave high school for college or university.

KEY IDEA FROM THIS STRATEGY

- Advocacy can be positive, neutral, or negative in nature.

- You will have to use all three types to ensure your ADHD success.

STRATEGY 12
BUILDING GREAT RELATIONSHIPS

Relationships and ADHD can be a difficult challenge. In the beginning, when you are involved with someone, they may marvel at your energy, enthusiastic personality, creativity, and spontaneous nature. This can get old quickly because of the consequences of these seemingly attractive traits. Let's examine each issue and how to handle them.

Boundless energy

Remember that your partner without ADHD may not appreciate that energy at 5 in the morning, or that your motor keeps running well into the night. Try to step away from your own energy and needs, and look at your partner. What is the feedback you are getting? It's not about changing who you are, but about understanding and appreciating their needs. Take the time to understand your partner's cycle of energy. Are they a morning or evening person? What is your cycle of energy? Are you using coffee or sugar to maintain your energy levels?

Pay attention

In couples therapy it is very common for the non-ADHD partner to complain that he/she never "seems to be listening to me or paying attention to my needs." This is often interpreted as disinterest in the relationship or an uncaring attitude. It may be that this is the case, but it may also be that ADHD symptoms and lack of focus are the true cause of the apparent disinterest.

It is also possible that you are able to listen to, and understand, all that your partner is saying even if you aren't looking at them. Get in the habit of making eye contact when talking to your partner. If you are having problems focusing while listening, say that. It isn't that you don't care or don't want to listen, but that right now you are a 9 out of 10 on the focus scale, and it's just not working. You may also have an impulse to ask for the short version of the discussion, but that likely won't be interpreted in a positive manner. Clear, honest, open communication with your partner about your focus level is essential. You will need to help them understand the difference between having a poor focus level and not caring about what they are saying. You may also then ask to talk about the issue after you go for a run or after you re-focus by taking a short walk.

Anger management

Emotions are often near the surface with ADHD, and anger is one of those. For temporal lobe ADHD this can be a particularly difficult issue. You will need to understand the levels of anger that you project, the impact of those on your partner, and what strategies you can employ to neutralize them.

If the number 1 means very relaxed and the number 10 very angry, little is accomplished once we are above a level 3 or 4. At this point, anger takes over, words are said, and you will likely forget the lessons of emotional IQ that we discussed in previous chapters. When you feel you are at a level 3 or 4, indicate that you need time and space. Separate yourself from the situation, engage in some form of exercise or self-reflection. Examine what button was pushed to cause your emotional response. Focus on what you want to get out of the discussion with your partner. Only return to the situation when you are calm and able to listen.

Listening to your partner

Listening can be a problem for those with ADHD. I mean *really* listening. This could be due to focus problems at the time, or perhaps undiagnosed central auditory processing difficulties or some other learning disability.

When you find yourself having problems listening to your partner, tell her that you very much want to listen to what she is saying, but are having problems focusing. It's not because you don't care— it's because of your focus level. Using the self-task focus rating system, it generally takes a level 4 or lower to truly focus and listen to your partner.

In a crisis, of course, emotions may override this focus issue and you will very quickly hone in to what your partner is saying.

Providing open, honest feedback is the key if you are having problems concentrating on a conversation. Your partner will have to let go of the topic if you indicate you want to discuss it at a later time or date. This can be challenging if she wants to get something resolved immediately.

KEY IDEA FROM THIS STRATEGY

- Your partner needs to understand the various symptoms of ADHD that you may be experiencing, and how this may affect your ability to focus, communicate, and attend to conversations.

- Anger management may be a problem, particularly if ADHD-temporal lobe type is involved. Work to understand the feelings that begin to happen as you get angry, learn strategies to reduce them, or learn to leave the situation before it becomes volatile. Indicate to your partner the need to walk away when this happens.

- Make sure you understand your partner's wake-sleep cycle. You may have boundless energy in the morning or late into the evening, which may not be compatible with their tolerance levels.

STRATEGY 13
EXERCISE

When we ask those with ADHD if exercise helps them control their symptoms, greater than 50 percent agree.

Exercise is an important strategy to use to improve your level of focus.

Before you start to use exercise, make sure your doctor gives you the green light, especially if you haven't been working out for some time. Cardio, increasing your heart rate during exercise, seems to trigger the good hormones and brain feeling that we all crave. Cardio exercise can lead to better focus and concentration for as long as sixty minutes.

What kind of workout?

If you visit a health club for an evaluation, your resting heart rate will likely be compared to your maximum heart rate as calculated by the professional. A target range will be determined and a program provided that will encourage you to exercise at least five times a week.

I prefer a home gym, or in my case a treadmill, so that it is convenient, easily accessible, and private. I wear a heart rate monitor for each workout and suggest you do the same. It is an immediate reward to have target heart rates—beats per minute (bpm)—to shoot for each workout. I work out in the mornings if my schedule allows. I can bring my level of focus to a 2 or 3 by doing my routine. All of my boring work gets accomplished immediately after my workout.

Your program will be different. We know that exercise can be helpful in treating many physical ailments, diseases, and can control ADHD. It is curative, releases anger, and helps us fight disease. So why is it still a common practice to deny children with ADHD recess, or activity, as a consequence of misbehaving?

All children with ADHD should exercise at least 60 minutes per day at school—30 minutes in the morning and 30 minutes in the afternoon to help maximize their performance in school.

Remember, we are talking about focused exercise, with a heart rate monitor to chart progress. Walking around at recess, or standing around and talking before the bell, isn't what we would call specific exercise for ADHD.

Just as with any treatment, the benefits of exercise and ADHD should be monitored. I have discussed the use of www.trackadhd.com and that would be my suggestion. Use this tool to monitor the effectiveness of exercise and ADHD.

KEY IDEA FROM THIS STRATEGY

- In excess of 50 percent of people with ADHD find that cardio exercise can improve focus and concentration.

- Have a professional design a program for you and use a cardiac monitor to help chart your success and give you immediate feedback.

- Children should never be denied activity or recess as a consequence of misbehaving.

STRATEGY 14
PARENTING YOUR ADHD CHILD

Parenting any child can be difficult today. Never before have parents faced such challenges and with fewer tools. The Internet allows children to have access to worlds and environments that can be hard for parents to control. The media has fewer rules and regulations so that young, underdeveloped minds can be easily exposed to negative images and stimulus.

Video games have also become much more realistic, bringing children into fantasy worlds at an ever-addicting pace. Children with ADHD are affected greatly by these environmental changes.

The rapid reinforcement and stimulating video or Internet world trains them to expect immediate rewards and gratification, something that is not often available in the classroom or real world.

As a parent, imposing discipline can be a confusing and frustrating experience. You want what is best for your child, but realize that this may mean providing logical consequences when your child misbehaves. Spanking, a tool used many years ago by parents, is rarely accepted today. In fact, in many jurisdictions spanking your child can be grounds for reporting you to the local children's aid society for investigation of child abuse.

So what should you do? I have provided a step-by-step approach to help you develop the structure and discipline you will need to help your child diagnosed with ADHD. Each child is different; these are not absolute rules. However, it will give you a better idea of ways you can encourage your child to find ADHD success.

Develop predictable routines

Early in your child's life you likely became aware of the need to develop predictable routines surrounding meal times and bed times. Those two events probably created your greatest challenges if you are parenting a child with ADHD.

Children with ADHD need a predictable schedule.

When they get up, when they eat, when they go to sleep, how to prepare them for sleep are all important parts of this structure and routine. As the parent, you need to establish this for your child. You don't ask them when they would like to eat or go to bed—you *tell* them. Children with ADHD, especially young children, do not have the ability to know when they should eat or go to bed. It is your job to decide.

A posted schedule of activity times is helpful for children. Post one in their room and one in the kitchen or some other prominent place.

Children with ADHD often suffer from fatigue throughout the day and need to eat healthy nutritious snacks whenever they are hungry. Do not deny them this.

What to do if your child refuses to eat at meal time

First, ask yourself have they been snacking an hour or so before dinner. If not, then simply tell your child you will put the food in the fridge and when they are hungry you will warm it for them. Don't get into a power struggle or demand that they eat it.

Monitor snack intake immediately prior to dinner. Your child will not be able to eat dessert, however, unless they eat some of the main course. If they come back to the table and protest when the family is eating that dessert, you may say, "I would love to give you dessert, but if you are hungry you need to eat the main course first."

Sleep routines

Children diagnosed with ADHD need to wind down before bedtime. There should be no video game playing, rough play, or adrenalin-pumping activity after 6 p.m. When easing your young child to sleep, tucking them in with a short, five-minute story is ideal; then leave the room. Your child should fall asleep within ten minutes. If this does not happen, adjust the time of bed time to your child's age. Never, and I mean never, allow your child to sleep with you or your spouse. It does not allow for a proper separation between your role as parent and partner, but also does not allow your child to achieve a proper sleep routine.

If your child is up at night, slowly walk them back to their bed, and again, do the five-minute routine and then leave them in their bed. Even if you have to do this many times, eventually your child will learn that this is the routine. As your child increases in age, place a lock on your bedroom door to further emphasize this boundary. Your child may knock if they need something, but unapproved access to your sleeping area is not allowed.

I know that for many of you this will be difficult, but for children with ADHD this is a crucial step in developing independence, positive self-esteem and self-image.

If they get up at night, gently walk them back to their own bed, reassure them that all is fine, stay for five minutes, then leave.

Discipline

If you think of discipline in any setting, you likely see it as an orderly environment where children do as they are told by adults who are in charge of the situation.

Children generally move from external cues and reminders of how to behave when they are young, to internal ones that will guide their behavior when you aren't there to enforce the rules.

If you are very strict with your children and give them little freedom they will have a difficult time handling total freedom those first few years away from home. If, however, you allow your child to behave as they would like, at all times, in all situations, you are teaching them that they will always get their way in life, and there is nothing they really have to do if they don't want to.

Children with ADHD need more structure and discipline than those without the diagnosis. Gradually, the majority of the rules will be internalized, but usually this is later than other children. Reward what you genuinely see as appropriate behavior and have tools to discourage inappropriate behavior and you will be well on your way.

What rewards?

When your child behaves appropriately, is thoughtful to others, respectful to adults, and helps a friend, make sure you give positive praise. Genuine, positive praise from a parent is very valuable and powerful. Often, it is the only tangible reward you need to provide. But do so in ample quantity when you "catch" your child doing the right thing.

What punishments?

When your child misbehaves you need to think of the following routine. This is a suggested process for a 10-year-old, but can be modified for any age.

Your child gets into a fight at recess, you get a call, and have to go to the school and pick him up. Once in the car, you say nothing; you let your emotions filter out without clouding your judgement. You simply tell your child you will talk about this in about an hour. Once home, you tell your child to go to their room so you can think and they can get their story together of what happened.

When you have calmed down, enter your child's room and ask them to tell you what happened. They will have from two to four minutes to tell their story. Next, ask them what they should do next time such an event occurs that would compel them to fight. If the answer is what you had in mind, thank your child for that answer, and ask them to try to do that next time. Lastly, you will need to provide a consequence to your child for their behavior.

Logical consequences could include a written apology to the other student, or even the teacher, for disrupting recess. Grounding could also be applied depending on the seriousness of the fight.

Grounding, or any consequence, should never extend to the next day unless the event is very serious and the child is 15 years of age or greater.

Grounding means regular meals and food, with no access to computers, other than supervised for school homework. No access to phones or video games or friends. Grounding means staying in their bedroom reading or engaging in some other quiet activity. When the grounding time is over, it is over.

Regardless of how you feel about the incident at school, you cannot let your child believe that you will go to school and fight with teachers or administrators to make it right. Your job is to advocate for your child, but not to let them know when you are doing so. If you feel you need to talk to the teacher or school about the incident, do so without your 10-year-old present, and indicate that you do not want them to tell your child you were at school advocating for your child. You must present a united front with the school that your child's behavior at recess was unacceptable.

Please remember that keeping your child from recess as a punishment by the school is not acceptable. As discussed, children with ADHD need to be active and exercise to improve school performance. Children also need practice getting along with others during free playtime at recess. Denying them the opportunity to interact with other children and learn from their mistakes is not going to improve that behavior. Denying a child recess due to their ADHD is a human rights issue and should be dealt with. In this example of fighting at recess, you, as a parent, have already dealt with the behavior, and your child should be allowed to attend the next day. You have done your job.

If your child has ADHD, you need to be comfortable with administering these sorts of punishments, but they should be logical in nature, meaning the punishment should be related to what happened.

A disagreement that results in an argument requires an apology and some form of restitution. The breaking of a window means extra work around the house to pay to fix it. Disrespecting a teacher would suggest restitution to the teacher for being disrespectful in the form of an apology letter, and to the class a verbal apology for disrupting the learning environment.

The goal is to encourage your child to internalize these types of consequences for misbehaving so that eventually they are performing them without the need for your prompting.

When it comes to discipline, it is your job as a parent to provide your child with the tools necessary to find their ADHD success. Each situation will differ based on your own experiences as a child, the severity of your child's ADHD, and the supports you have available. Don't be afraid to ask for help. From an experienced parent (grandmother or grandfather) to a health care professional, such as a psychologist, don't be afraid to ask, especially when you forget to catch your child doing the right things.

Weekly quality one-on-one time

If your child is two years of age to an older teen, right now go to the calendar and pencil in a date and time where you will spend thirty minutes with your child in a one-on-one situation. Just you and your child. No one else. Not your spouse, not the other children. Not your cell phone or newspapers—just you and your child. What you do cannot be competitive. No video games, although for much older teens that would be fine just to have some time with them.

On the appointed time and date, provide some activities or materials (for younger children), or engage in an activity that the older child may have requested. Simply play with your child. Observe them at first, listen to them. Never take this time away because of behavior or homework not being done, or anything else. It is time with your child that is not contingent on them displaying anything.

You are providing unconditional quality time with them. You love them for who they are and you will demonstrate this fifty-two times a year during this special one-on-one time.

I have written a course for parents that can be taken online called "Parenting Your ADHD Child." For a free preview and the video on discipline go to www.drsvec.com.

KEY IDEA FROM THIS STRATEGY

- Creating structure in your home for young children with ADHD is focused on meal and bed times.

- Using logical consequences for acting out is suggested.

- The goal is to move your child from external structures and rewards to internal ones.

- Thirty minutes of quality one-on-one time weekly with you and your child should be part of any discipline strategy. This is not contingent on your child's behavior.

STRATEGY 15
ACCEPTING YOUR ADHD SUCCESS

If you have ADHD you have likely learned early in life how to deal with failure. At first, as a child, you may have gotten angry, frustrated, and lashed out when things didn't go your way. Later on, you may have wondered if things would ever go your way. You learned to overcome obstacles that seemed insurmountable because of the odds stacked against you. When you did experience some levels of success, you likely found it difficult to handle. You were excited and happy, but wondered what would happen next because things can't keep going well for you.

Accepting loss, frustration, and barriers becomes a way of life. Eventually, that is what you are used to. I will never forget one of my first depressed patients I was working with while doing my internship at a hospital many years ago. This person told me that living with depression became normal. It was much easier to face failure and lie in bed all day with the sheets over his head because no one had any expectations of success, there was no pressure, that rock bottom was comforting.

Like that, having ADHD can lead you or your child to a life of expecting failure and even searching it out. You understand failure; you know how to deal with that. But what happens if you follow the advice I've given you in this book, work at the skills and strategies, and experience success beyond your wildest dreams as a parent, partner, business person, or professional? Here's what will start to happen as you experience success.

Self-change: what happened to me?

You will have to confront any past ADHD failures that still stand out and stop you from moving forward and accepting success. It was a step I had to take not that long ago.

I have been involved in the business of psychology for the past twenty years. It is hard, focused work in a profession with little history of creativity or marketing savvy. Very early in the game I realized that the majority of the public do not know what we do as psychologists. So I started to tell the public. I took out radio ads, the back cover of the phone books, television ads, newspaper ads, any way that I could scream out to the public what my profession could do, I did.

It took work, it took time to review my early life experiences with success and failure, but over the few months of work I learned to accept and live with success. I learned that living with failure was part of my ADHD life experience, so much so that rarely had I enjoyed success, or learned to handle it. Success had occurred just as it does for you, but I wasn't seeing it. But remember, I didn't perceive the success that was there. Guilt, a sense of being unworthy, not talented enough, not good enough, were messages I had constantly been telling myself—messages that others had also delivered, and quite effectively.

Learning to live with your success will take some work. You will need to do some self-reflection, review how you truly feel when things go well, or perhaps have time with a coach, or as I did, psychologist. Accept that it is something you will need to change starting today; a change that will help you discover your ADHD success.

Accept, too, that many of your friends will have a hard time accepting the new you. They will leave you or perhaps even try to sabotage your success. Your new rule is to only be around those that will encourage you and be happy for your success, success as a spouse or partner. Success as a mother or father. Success as a professional or business owner. Each of these will be within your grasp. Remember, however, that success doesn't mean buying all the physical objects that scream out "Look at me. I can buy things you can't." Living with ADHD success is about an internal level of confidence that has nothing to do with your physical possessions or status.

I drive old cars and buy them used. Mind you it may be a Volvo or Mercedes, but they are not bought new, bought at least one or two years old because those are the best deals. I live in the same house with my wife that we built twenty years ago on our farm. We will live there, hopefully, until the day they carry us out. I buy clothes maybe once a year, if forced to by my wife. We enjoy time at home together and go to our condo up north as a vacation. Occasionally, we travel, but rarely. As I tell many of my friends, you can live quite comfortably in Blenheim, Ontario on a modest income. It is true. We have one amazing coffee shop that really should be in East Lansing, Michigan or Boston or Toronto, but for some reason ended up in my small hometown. We have two stop lights. I like being a big fish in a little pond.

The best way I can describe living with ADHD success and learning to accept it as an adult is that each day for me is like Christmas. When I wake up in the morning, I can't wait to get at it. It's like that anticipation you may have had as a child that Christmas morning or before Hanukkah—just can't wait to get started and find out what the day will bring.

KEY IDEA FROM THIS STRATEGY

- Living with your ADHD success may require you to seek out the assistance of a coach or psychologist. Are you able to truly feel the joy of your success?

- Some of your friends will leave you as you become more successful. Learn to accept this.

PUTTING IT ALL TOGETHER

My hope is that the strategies I have outlined in this book will help you achieve your ADHD success. It will take work, but as you start to see change, momentum will build.

I truly believe that by focusing on the specific skills you need to develop, you will start to see success within three to six months. Within one year as an adult with ADHD, you will begin to feel the wind brush by as you surpass even your own wildest expectations for life enjoyment.

For children, knowing how to overcome ADHD symptoms will be extremely valuable in preserving self-esteem. The self-task matching exercise is vital in helping them understand the need to monitor their own levels of focus. Fully understanding their diagnosis in a language they can understand is also vital. Building a toolbox of successful strategies is the goal. Each day they must have an opportunity to work on their gifts. Focus on those abilities and skills, not the areas of weakness. Use strategies to overcome deficits, but also use them to enhance greatness.

Find your ADHD success. Start today.

Finding my ADHD Success: Josh's Story

My name is Joshua Svec and I have been diagnosed with ADHD. To me, ADHD is not what defines me. ADHD is a label, and that label is used to explain to those that need explaining that I do things a little differently than most people. But to me there is nothing wrong with that. Doing things different is what defines all of us; doing things different is human.

My first experience with ADHD came at an early age. It was in grade school that I realized it took me a lot longer to accomplish daily assignments than my peers. I went through a psychological evaluation and was diagnosed with ADHD. The process that followed the diagnosis was an important stage in my life. I went through a biofeedback program and also received coaching on the best strategies for me to accomplish my schoolwork and homework effectively. These tools became the building blocks for my entire academic career, and I was fortunate to receive early diagnosis and support.

High school was difficult for me. I felt the majority of the teachers at my high school did not care about the individual student, but lectured to the class. I look back on my high school experience with teachers and I am glad to have experienced people like that at an early age in my academic career. There will be people who don't care for you in all aspects of your life.

I learned in high school that in order for me to be successful in academics, I had to rely on myself. I dealt with teachers who didn't care, didn't think my worth was anything, and who took pleasure in seeing me fail. But the lesson I learned was that there will always be people like that in your life. It is important to recognize who they are so that they don't interfere with your personal goals and success.

I attended the University of Waterloo where I was enrolled in the Bachelor of Arts program for psychology, and where I played varsity football. I also registered with the Office of Persons with Disability (OPD) to receive accommodations on my exams. These accommodations included my own room to write tests and a computer to type my written answers on for essay questions during examinations.

In order for me to succeed in my daily schoolwork at university, I had to be organized. I worked out my class schedule to be mainly morning classes, giving me two to three hours a day after my classes were finished to hit the library and complete chapter readings, assignments, or study before my football practise began. I did this because I knew that after practise I would be too tired to complete any school work. This also gave me time to relax before the next day. Sticking to this timeframe was very important for me. I was determined to get my work done in that two to three hour time slot after my classes. Being in an undergraduate degree majoring in psychology, the majority of my homework time was put towards chapter readings. With study tips from the University of Waterloo's Office for Persons with Disability, I started reading five pages at a time with a break in between. But most of the time, I only made it to two to three pages before needing a break.

The first two years of university were a learning process for me in terms of my own personal ways to study and succeed. It was in my second year that I had to battle to gain entry into the honors psychology program. In order to be in the honors program I needed a 75 percent in my psychology classes, and a 70 percent in the remainder of my classes, or my elective classes. In order to achieve this goal, I needed to get an 83 percent average in my psychology classes and around a 75 percent in my electives. I have never had an average that high before. I remember that entire term I was motivated to achieve my goal. I structured my days to the last minute, organizing what pages I would read, and how much time I had to complete my work. I always gave myself more time than what was needed. I never completed everything I set out to complete in one work session, but it didn't matter to me because I would set enough time for me to allow myself to finish my work early, sometimes allotting a two-hour slot to read ten pages. I knew what I could handle and I didn't put any pressure on myself.

I wrote out my goals and put them in a spot in my room that I could see every day. I wrote out the exact grades I wanted to achieve for each class. My family background and history also helped motivate me, and I wrote out "they want you to fail" and placed it above my desk. It was important for me to visually see my goals. I woke up every day with a game plan and had the tools to follow that game plan.

My grades were always highest during the term my sport's season was in. I believe this is because during the football season I was the most organized. I had to be in order to accomplish my work.

Football was a way for me to release my anger and frustration from my day in a healthy atmosphere. I loved football. If I had any problem throughout my day with school or assignments, or anxiety with upcoming tests, I would be able to let it all go at practise. I treated practise like games and went all out. I came to Waterloo a nobody, not recruited by universities coming out of high school, basically a walk on. I left the team's most valuable player, team captain, conference all-star, and the team record holder for most receiving yards in a single season. There was no secret to my success here. I just worked hard and loved what I did. No one knew I had ADHD. I did extra things no one saw in order to maintain my focus on the field. Mental visualization was huge for me in university sports. It allowed me to get mental reps any time of the day.

In my university career there came a time when I could have taken a path that to me seemed like cheating, in both academics and athletics. Being on a varsity football team with over a hundred people on the roster, you are placed in a room at an early age with people you have never met before, which is a great experience. However, it places you with people who you may not usually be friends with in your own personal life. As a young man, I saw people who had taken the quick fix, or cheat to get ahead.

For example, in academics, students could have self-medicated themselves with prescribed medications in order to focus and study. In athletics, students could have been using steroids to get ahead on the field. I have never believed or used these types of quick fixes. I knew that if I worked hard I would reach my goals. I believe I stayed true to that value because I knew strategies to be successful. In football, I believed in my coaches, and knew the best player would play; it was as simple as that. In order to be the best player, I had to work hard.

In academics, I was fortunate enough to be given personal strategies to succeed in school at an early age. Those strategies evolved over time with the help of others, such as OPD in university. If you work hard to achieve your goal, and believe every day that you are working towards that goal, you will accomplish what you set out to do. Believe in yourself and the unique qualities you have.

I got to a point where my strategies for success became automatic. Just when you figure things out and get a grasp on things, you have to move on to new experiences. Just when I felt comfortable and was succeeding, my four years of my undergraduate career were completed.

Currently, my ADHD is personally more noticeable than ever before. I have just graduated from the University of Western Ontario with a Master in Arts in Kinesiology and I have decided to take some time off from any serious commitments. I am currently employed in a couple of odd jobs with various hours. The most noticeable difference in my life now from university is the lack of daily structure. I no longer have the previous goals in my life to shoot for (grades and football). This transition stage in my life reminds me that I must always be evolving, always learning how to be successful with ADHD. ADHD has not stopped me from achieving any of my previous goals, and it won't stop me from conquering my future goals.

My personal keys to success living with ADHD

Set goals

- Short-term and long-term goals.
- Can be anything, an important assignment at work or a major paper in school.
- Write them out so you can physically see them every day.

Stay organized

- Carry around a day planner or schedule to keep organized day to day.
- This is a minor way of setting daily goals, checking off your tasks as your complete them.

Always be open to new strategies

- This is more for academics.
- Be open to try new ways of observing information suggested to you by your life coach, psychologist, or academic supervisor.

Have a healthy outlet

- Exercise or play sports.

Always make time to be social

- Remember to enjoy life and have fun in the company of others.

APPENDIX A
OFFICIAL DIAGNOSTIC CRITERIA OF ADHD

A. Either (1) or (2)

1) Six or more of the following symptoms of **inattention** have persisted for at least six months to a degree that is maladaptive and inconsistent with the developmental level:

Inattention

1. often fails to give close attention to details or makes careless mistakes in schoolwork, work, or other activities
2. often has difficulty sustaining attention in tasks or play activities
3. often does not seem to listen when spoken to directly
4. often does not follow through on instructions and fails to finish schoolwork, chores, or duties in the workplace (not due to oppositional behavior or failure of comprehension)
5. often has difficulty organizing tasks and activities
6. often avoids, dislikes, or is reluctant to engage in tasks that require sustained mental effort (such as schoolwork or homework)
7. often loses things necessary for tasks or activities at school or at home (e.g. toys, pencils, books, assignments)
8. is often easily distracted by extraneous stimuli
9. if often forgetful in daily activities

2) Six or more of the following symptoms of **hyperactivity-impulsivity** have persisted for at least 6 months to a degree that is maladaptive and inconsistent with the developmental level:

Hyperactivity

1. often fidgets with hands or feet or squirms in seat
2. often leaves seat in classroom or in other situations in which remaining seated is expected
3. often runs about or climbs excessively in situations in which it is inappropriate (in adolescents or adults, may be limited to subjective feelings of restlessness)
4. often has difficulty playing or engaging in leisure activities quietly
5. often talks excessively
6. is often 'on the go' or often acts as if 'driven by a motor'

Impulsivity

1. often has difficulty awaiting turn in games or group situations
2. often blurts out answers to questions before they have been completed
3. often interrupts or intrudes on others, e.g. butts into other children's games

B. Some hyperactivity - impulsive or inattentive symptoms that cause impairment were present before the age of 7 years.

C. Some impairment from the symptoms is present in more than two or more settings (e.g. at school or work or at home).

D. There must be clear evidence of clinically significant impairment in social, academic, or occupational functioning.

E. The symptoms do not occur exclusively during the course of a Pervasive Developmental Disorder, Schizophrenia, or other Psychotic Disorder, and are not better accounted for by another mental disorder (e.g., Mood Disorder, Anxiety Disorder, Dissociative Disorder, or a Personality Disorder).

Based on these criteria, three types of ADHD are identified:

1. ADHD, Combined Type: if both criteria 1A and 1B are met for the past 6 months
2. ADHD, Predominantly Inattentive Type: if criterion 1A is met but criterion 1B is not met for the past six months
3. ADHD, Predominantly Hyperactive-Impulsive Type: if Criterion 1B is met but Criterion 1A is not met for the past six months.

The above information has been printed from the American Psychiatric Association: Diagnostic and Statistical Manual of Mental Disorders, Fourth Edition, Text Revision. Washington, DC, American Psychiatric Association, 2000.

APPENDIX B
ATTENTION DEFICIT DISORDER (ADD) SEVERITY SCALE—ATHLETES

By Dr. Henry J. Svec www.drsvec.com

1. Has difficulty remaining seated while not participating (fidgets or squirms on the bench or during travel)
Never 1 2 3 4 5 6 7 8 9 10–Almost always

2. Easily distracted during games or practice
Never 1 2 3 4 5 6 7 8 9 10–Almost always

3. Has difficulty waiting for his/her turn to participate
Never 1 2 3 4 5 6 7 8 9 10–Almost always

4. Often blurts our inappropriate comments during group activities or locker room times
Never 1 2 3 4 5 6 7 8 9 10–Almost always

5. Has problems following coach's instructions
Never 1 2 3 4 5 6 7 8 9 10–Almost always

6. Has difficulty focusing attention on a task during practice, games, or competition
Never 1 2 3 4 5 6 7 8 9 10–Almost always

7. Becomes bored with the sport after brief experience or
exposure
Never 1 2 3 4 5 6 7 8 9 10–Almost always

8. Experiences extreme fluctuations in performance
(outstanding one day, but quite poor the next, extreme case
compared with other players
Never 1 2 3 4 5 6 7 8 9 10–Almost always

9. Often forgets equipment needed to participate
Never 1 2 3 4 5 6 7 8 9 10–Almost always

10. .Often engages in physically dangerous play, more than
expected in the sport and in comparison to other athletes
Never 1 2 3 4 5 6 7 8 9 10–Almost always

APPENDIX C
ATTENTION DEFICIT DISORDER (ADD) SEVERITY SCALE— CHILDREN/ADOLESCENTS

By Dr. Henry J. Svec – www.drsvec.com

Choose the number that best describes your child's attention or behavior difficulties at school

1. Often fidgets or squirms in seat

Never   1   2   3   4   5   6   7   8   9   **10 – Severe**

2. Has difficulty remaining seated

Never   1   2   3   4   5   6   7   8   9   **10 – Severe**

3. Is easily distracted

Never   1   2   3   4   5   6   7   8   9   **10 – Severe**

4. Difficulty waiting for his/her turn

Never   1   2   3   4   5   6   7   8   9   **10 – Severe**

5. Often blurts out answers to questions

Never   1   2   3   4   5   6   7   8   9   **10 – Severe**

6. Has difficulty following instructions

Never   1   2   3   4   5   6   7   8   9   **10 – Severe**

7. Has difficulty keeping attention to task

Never   1   2   3   4   5   6   7   8   9   10 – Severe

8. Often shifts from one uncompleted task to another

Never   1   2   3   4   5   6   7   8   9   10 – Severe

9. Often loses things needed for tasks

Never   1   2   3   4   5   6   7   8   9   10 – Severe

10. Often engages in physically dangerous activities without considering consequences

Never   1   2   3   4   5   6   7   8   9   10 – Severe

Choose the number that best describes your child's behavior or attention difficulties at home

1. While playing with other children
Never 1 2 3 4 5 6 7 8 9 **10–Severe**

2. Mealtimes
Never 1 2 3 4 5 6 7 8 9 **10–Severe**

3. Getting dressed
Never 1 2 3 4 5 6 7 8 9 **10–Severe**

4. When visitors are in your home
Never 1 2 3 4 5 6 7 8 9 **10–Severe**

5. When you are visiting someone else
Never 1 2 3 4 5 6 7 8 9 **10–Severe**

6. At church or Sunday school
Never 1 2 3 4 5 6 7 8 9 **10–Severe**

7. In supermarkets, stores, restaurants, or other public places
Never 1 2 3 4 5 6 7 8 9 **10–Severe**

8. When asked to do chores at home
Never 1 2 3 4 5 6 7 8 9 **10–Severe**

9. While in the car
Never 1 2 3 4 5 6 7 8 9 **10–Severe**

10. When asked to do school homework
Never 1 2 3 4 5 6 7 8 9 10–Severe

APPENDIX D
ADHD SEVERITY SCALE—ADULTS

By Dr. Henry J. Svec – www.drsvec.com

Rate each of the following and then comment on each.

1. Problems organizing tasks at work or school
Never 1 2 3 4 5 6 7 8 9 **10–Always**

2. Problems remembering things
Never 1 2 3 4 5 6 7 8 9 **10–Always**

3. In meetings or in class problems sitting still or fidgeting
Never 1 2 3 4 5 6 7 8 9 **10–Always**

4. Problem completing boring tasks
Never 1 2 3 4 5 6 7 8 9 **10–Always**

5. Problems concentration when listening to others
Never 1 2 3 4 5 6 7 8 9 **10–Always**

6. Losing things needed for tasks
Never 1 2 3 4 5 6 7 8 9 **10–Always**

7. Problems staying seated during meetings or school lectures
Never 1 2 3 4 5 6 7 8 9 **10–Always**

8. Talking too much in social situations
Never   1   2   3   4   5   6   7   8   9   10–Always

9. Interrupting others at the wrong time in social situations or
meetings
Never   1   2   3   4   5   6   7   8   9   10–Always

10. Problems concentrating or focusing for expected periods of
time
Never   1   2   3   4   5   6   7   8   9   10–Always

11. Difficulty with anger or frustrating
Never   1   2   3   4   5   6   7   8   9   10–Always

12. Problems with self-esteem
Never   1   2   3   4   5   6   7   8   9   10–Always

13. Depression
Never   1   2   3   4   5   6   7   8   9   10–Always

14. Problems paying attention to spouse or partner in social
situations
Never   1   2   3   4   5   6   7   8   9   10–Always

15. Often will self-medication with coffee or other substances to
try to focus
Never   1   2   3   4   5   6   7   8   9   10–Always

HELPFUL WEBSITES

To look up medications for ADHD:
www.nlm.nih.gov/medlineplus/druginformation.html

Free site to track changes in ADHD symptoms:
www.trackadhd.com

Free site to track goals and practice the self-task strategy:
www.goaltracker.ca

Dr. Svec Institute where you can learn more on neurofeedback:
www.drsvec.com

Free video seminar with Dr. Svec on discipline in the home:
www.drsvec.com

www.ingramcontent.com/pod-product-compliance
Lightning Source LLC
Chambersburg PA
CBHW061732020426
42331CB00006B/1217